Jones Studio Houses

Sensual Modernism

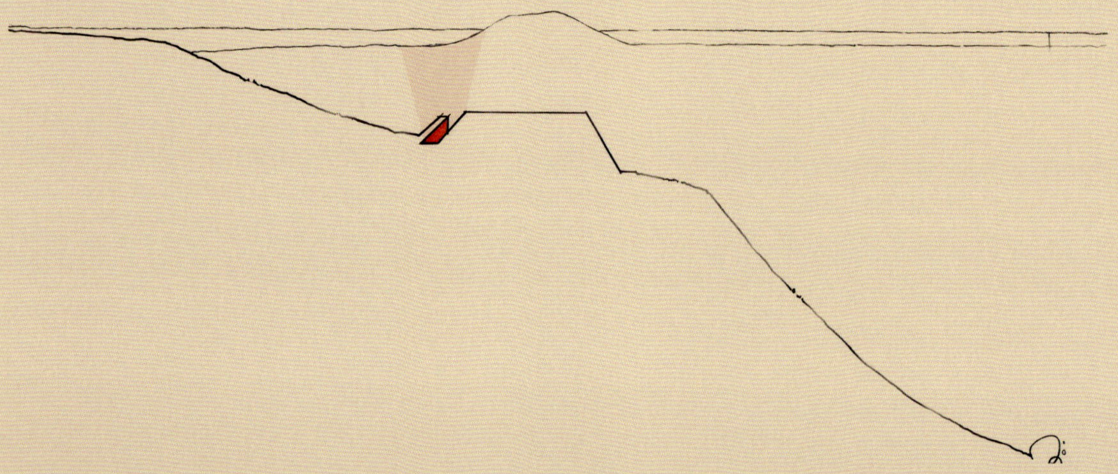

Jones Studio Houses

Sensual Modernism

Introduction
by Aaron Betsky

Interview
by Vladimir Belogolovsky

Epilogue
by Eddie Jones

OSCAR RIERA OJEDA
PUBLISHERS

Dedicaton to My Partners

Neal E. Jones, who made it real and took the bullets.

Jacob Benyi, nickname “ON STAR”, for his dazzling instant recall.

Brian Farling, most famous unknown architect in the Southwest.

Lisa Johnson, my wife, my best friend.
“She, who makes all things possible.”

CONTENTS

Introduction

by Aaron Betsky

Hover
The Architecture of Eddie Jones

The image above right presents a dream of what modern life in the desert might be. A pool of water hovers over a desert slope you can barely see in the gloaming of the light. Its blue shape meanders through the drawing as a human-made river. Fragmented horizontal planes hover above sections of glass window wall that march off into the sunset. There is just a hint of an interior life, but the view is out to the ancient and strange landscape. A saguaro cactus stands guard, acting as the focal point of the whole composition. This is life in the Sonoran Desert as Eddie Jones imagines it should play out.

It is the contrast between the vertical cactus, as well as the mountains in the background, and the plane that allows us to stand – or float, in the case of the pool – and be sheltered, that marks what Eddie Jones is best at doing. Always his floors tumble, twist, intersect, and spread. Always his roofs spread out above, making possible inhabitation that hovers above, but is still of, the desert landscape.

Jones' vision of domestic life in, but not quite of that landscape of sloping planes of boulders, abrupt interruptions of steep and barren hills, and rivers meandering through the flat planes at the base of these vertical places so inimical to human inhabitation hovers somewhere between dream and reality as the whole city in which he lives and works seems to never quite touch down. Eddie Jones' architecture is one of a rough limbo, fed just enough by technology, accepting of heat, the scorpions, and social isolation of the place, and luxurious without being indolent.

While human beings once hewed close to the many rivers that make this Valley one giant oasis, extending the habitable terrain with canals and migrating over the centuries with the water, and Western settlers then created courtyard houses or air conditioned boxes, Jones and his fellow desert modernists have chosen a different strategy: to rise slightly above it all, while remaining rooted; to open up to the environment, while providing shelter defined by forms and materials whose weight is an abstraction of the desert itself; and to rotate, twist, and skewer all those forms together into compounds whose sprawl provides moments of light and shade, light and dark, and large and small space.

I say "Jones and his fellow modernists" because Eddie Jones does not work alone. He works, first of all, with his office, and in particular with his brother Neal. He also acknowledges the work in particular of Frank Lloyd Wright and some of that Wisconsin transplant's followers and collaborators, whose approach to the Southwest desert was rather idiosyncratic. He points out the work of artists such as James Turrell, who have taken that same landscape to a level of abstraction and intensity that no architect has ever been able to achieve. Certainly, his own upbringing in Oklahoma, both in terms of the particularities of its prairie landscape and in the presence of the work of Bruce Goff, Herb Greene, Bart Prince, and other architects of what has come to be called the "American School," have been important factors in how his work has developed, giving him a sense of strangeness and allowing him to continue to marvel at the desert.

But Eddie Jones is also an heir to the particular adaptation of the orthogonal and minimal planes, preferably carried out in glass, steel, and concrete, that European modernists developed before the

Second World War and that the architects who were part of L.A.'s Case Study program then adapted to the American social, economic, and physical landscape. Jones is a modernist, not interested in quoting or repeating, but rather seeking to reinvent what it means to be alive in modernity.

It is in the work of the Case Study's Phoenix pupils and associates, such as Al Beadle, Calvin Straub, and Ralph Haver, that the roots of Eddie Jones' work lie. It is these architects who figured out how an idiom developed first in the temperate zones of Europe and then in the forgiving coastal climate of California could adapt to the Sonoran Desert. By paying attention to the sun and its direction, acknowledging the need to shelter in the desert through the use of heavy counterpoints to the glass and steel planes, and by creating compounds of complex forms that began to answer to the expressive complexity of the desert, these architects developed an idiom in which great architects such as not only Jones, but also slightly older colleagues such as Will Bruder and two generations of Jack DeBartolos, as well as younger ones such as Wendell Burnette and Rick Joy, could unfold their forms.

Within this tradition, Eddie Jones has developed his own way of working, formal vocabulary, and compositional sense. The basic building blocks of this practice are simple and even reductive. First, of course, there are the elements that have by now become the signals of a certain kind of modernity. These include flat roofs (although Jones does not always use those, particularly when he works elsewhere); vertical planes of glass that are as large as possible, have as few seams as the architect can manage, and seem to hover in place; that sense of floating, which inscribes the structure as a geometric figure in the landscape; and an interior composition that emphasizes the openness of spaces, minimizing any cellular division and, when separations and portals are necessary, tries to equate the windows and doors as much as possible with the scale, and materials of the walls.

Then there are the materials, which include not only the glass and steel that allows the architect to carry out the work described above, but also concrete, which Jones uses to contrast with these lighter planes, and, what is more significant, various forms of rammed earth that are not only more ecological sensible, but also allow Jones' structures to continue a native tradition while building with more or less local materials. Jones also uses more eccentric materials, including wood slats cut at random to create patterns and syncopations in rooms and on facades, and brass pieces used not for flashing or even necessarily as decoration, but as elements that also add a different scale, rhythm, and texture to the otherwise often minimal houses.

That sense of syncopation is in fact central to many of Jones' best compositions. It is what gives his architecture its particular style, in a more fundamental manner than the expressive gestures he sometimes adds to his buildings. This is true both spatially, in the mix of small and large rooms that also can be heavy or light, and in terms of the weaving together of abstraction and gestural forms themselves. Gestures, which include arches, bows, and curves, are also common in Jones' work, although he shares this particularity with Will Bruder and, ultimately with much of Frank Lloyd Wright's late work. I have to admit that they are not my favorite part of his designs, but it is their integration into the orthogonal framework of most of his houses that makes Jones' uses of these elements particular and successful.

Finally, there is the contrast between enigmatic and figurative elements that plays through Jones' best designs. Eddie Jones seems to veer back and forth between clouding the clarity of the minimalist forms in which he works, most explicitly through the use of translucent and colored glass, and creating references, whether to a tradition of building with arches in Mexico or to Herb Greene's Prairie Chicken House in his "Raptor" project in Oklahoma. In that sense, he is a Post-modernist, promiscuous in his use of whatever form, element, material, or composition he thinks will serve his design best.

This particularity also means Eddie Jones' work exhibits a surprising amount of variety even when he works on a limited range of commissions (the bulk of his residential work consists of the design of houses for wealthy patrons) in a limited geographic area (though he has also worked, beyond Oklahoma and Mexico, in California, in Montana, and in other parts of the Rocky Mountains) with a limited palette of materials. Whereas the previous generation of modernists stayed within one set of forms for most of their life, and other architects of Jones' generation have made shifts in their work over time, this architect seems to adapt his mode of working to one particular situation or another, moving back and forth between boxes and circles, heavy and light, and expressive and recessive forms depending on the situation.

What Eddie Jones achieves with such complexity is a specificity in the work that at the same time has a sense of openness and clarity. Take his own office, for example. A box that sits at the edge of its lot, it appears to be just another contribution to the parade of such forms through the plains of the Salt River. Then Jones adds a crown of seemingly colored glass, which already throws off our understanding of what the building is, as well as an expectation of proportion we might have. He then punctures the concrete block pattern with random openings, and, around the entrance corner, dissolves it into a freestanding screen wall. Color and light pierce the volume. Make your way into the space and what appears to be just a loft building, its ceiling angled up to catch the south light, is filled with moments of level changes, planes jutting out, and slight variations to what appears to be a simple volume. All of this creates something between a studio and an abstract composition of geometries, open to the landscaped courtyard, but sheltered from both the humanmade and the natural reality around the building.

Such a play is also on display at the Logan House, which doubles as a home for one of the Southwest's best private collections of contemporary art. There the contrast is one between solid and void above all else. The concrete that forms the house's structure becomes either solid or planar, opening up to large and light-filled interior spaces while also anchoring the house to the slope on which it perches. You tumble down the site and move out to its views in ways that draw you both in and out. Jones even punctures the ceiling of the main atrium, which is both the central circulation and party space and a gallery, with a grid of skylights to point out this contrast of interwoven planes, while confusing what is inside and what is outside.

What makes the complexity of these homes work is the simplicity of their basic organization, more often than not one that Jones derives either from Frank Lloyd Wright's Prairie Style homes or his later, curved domiciles. In the former case, he inscribes an "X" on the landscape, as he does in the Outpost House, siting the composition's heart not in the center of living, but as the void where two (or more) patterns of circulation cross and devolve the house. The whole house, in fact, seems to be little more than an intersection, leaving the solids and the structure hidden from the public spaces behind slats and screens. In the latter case, the arch is an embrace of the view and leaning back into the landscape.

The Outpost House is Jones' most overt homage to Frank Lloyd Wright's work, as the house relates directly to one of that architect's lost masterpieces (on a nearby site), the so-called Shiprock or Pauson House of 1940, but also because of the manner in which he has here fully realized the fluidity between inside and outside that is so central to Wright's best work. The house's main living space is cave built into the top of the slope that is completely open to the Valley below. Like the Anasazi dwellings built into the sides of mesas, the Outpost House both shelters and provides a sense of surveillance. The rammed earth walls make it even more part of the site, while the lines of the walls and the swimming pool, which stand at angles to this anchoring background, key into distant mountains. Caught between these two sets of lines, one of refuge and prospect, one of connection, the house's other spaces, both inside and outside, nestle like what Jones, in a pun on his first name, calls "eddies" that also reflect his own continual attempts to make sense of and capture the wide open desert landscape in his work.

Against such a bias to create a unitary gesture that then devolves into an assembly of Jones' stock-in-trade elements adapted to a particular site, there is also a tendency in Eddie Jones' buildings exhibit to fall apart into pavilions. This transformation of a house into separate parts, each with its own center and roof, is most clear in the home he designed in Montana, but it is also latent in his own house on South Mountain. It is that continual picking apart at the scale not only of walls, rooms, and bits and pieces (like those wood slats), but also as far as the whole building goes, that keeps Jones' designs light and complex, coherent and expansive at the same time.

While most of Jones' work relies on rectilinear forms to contrast with and define a relation towards the natural landscape, he also has a love of curves, diagonals, and expressive gestures that sweep out towards views while grabbing onto natural features such as rock piles or creek beds. The most expressive of the houses that exhibit these tendencies is the house he calls, appropriately enough, the Scorpion. It is one curve, looking, like most of the architect's houses, out over the landscape below, that then repeats itself in fragmented curves of roofs and walls that move out and back into the site. The lines emanate from an inverted conical roof over the living room, which provides both shelter and a sense of center. Segmented glass walls erase the line between inside and out. Bedrooms, a study, and a guest pavilion claw their way out into crevasses between the boulders, letting light slot in through fragments of windows and clerestories between the roof plane. Jones likes to think of his houses as animals (an osprey in Mexico, a raptor in Oklahoma), but also as high tech slivers slotted into the landscape. The Scorpion brings this notion of architecture as something alien that is still part of both the humanmade and the natural landscape to its highest refinement.

Nowhere does all of this come together in a stranger and more satisfying manner than in what the architect calls The House of Five Dreams. If there is a reference in this design, it is surely, however, not to Morpheus, but to an iceberg. The building's bulk exists underground, as private warehouse for another vast collection that, however, is made up of pieces that are both smaller and more delicate. When you enter into the house, you can either descend into this other realm, where Jones has kept his tendency to float planes and hover forms to a minimum, and which is, therefore, one of the most dramatic and enclosed volumes he has allowed himself to design, or you can ascend up to the main house on a glass staircase.

There you find yourself indeed floating into world that could be made of ice and mist, somehow transported to or, rather, over the desert. Not only the walls are made out of glass, but so are some of the floors and ceilings. The curves or gestures are not solid, but consist of curtains that weave in and out of the walls. The sun is kept at bay not with overhangs and orientation, but with a fabric wrapper that pivots out from the bottom, so that the building emerges in its transparency from its translucent shell. I can imagine that all of Eddie Jones' architecture could be like this: an enigma in which light dissolves and carves spaces that resist definition and even touch with levels of clarity and opacity that are belied by the path you cut through them, creating moments of sense and others of sensuality, mixed and arranged in space in such a way as to build gentle surprise into the patterns of everyday life.

It is a shame that this book concentrates almost wholly on Eddie Jones' residential work. True, it is here that he has been most able to experiment, as is the case with most American architects. However, he has also shown himself to be a very good architect of civic structures, as his office would already indicate. His renovation of a former multiplex cinema into the Mesa Community College Art Center shows his ability to create beauty even with very simple materials, on a difficult site and, what is most important, within an existing building. Similarly, his designs for the Cococino and Mohave Community Colleges show his ability to use his roofs to denote and carry the sense of community, leaving minimal interruptions and gradations of scale to define the activities within these spaces. The Glulam beams of the latter building in particular are one of his most expressive statements of the hover (without using expressive shapes) I have seen in his work.

Even better as a design than that of these small school structures is the one for the Mariposa Border Crossing, which is as much of a statement of essences as the House of Five Dreams. Here Jones has folded and unfolded the line of demarcation between the United States and Mexico – a simple fact whose social implications are anything but that – into the housing for all the apparatus that maintains that political fiction. In so doing he has created an open scaffolding that does just enough to shelter the users from the sun, and is just open enough to allow for security sight lines, but also heavy enough to resist attack. The whole of the construction becomes less of a building than a continual set of intersections and, again, hovering planes of canopies and slats that define space, dapple light, and create continuity against these moments of control and intimidating inspection.

Jones has proposed larger structures, such as his version of Wright's Price Tower, which he sees as a vertical emblem and motor of densification in the Valley of the Sun's sprawl. This structure is also a vertical version of his houses, its always hovering, cantilevered planes becoming boxes for living as well as solids mixing with gardened voids, while the whole balances out from a central mast. It is no accident, I believe, that Eddie Jones decided to close the volume at hand with this image, which so closely mirrors the saguaro standing sentinel at the beginning of the book. He has learned from nature and turned it into an urban element. The promise of such an intervention is strong, and I can only hope that he will have the chance to develop the craft he has honed so expertly at the domestic level at such a scale.

There are no universal truths we can learn from Eddie Jones. There are also very few tricks we can pick up (other than his way of drawing, which draws out from the pencil all the expressive potential of which it is capable). His work is too specific to site, client, and occasion. It is also a work that is based on the craft of combining materials and forms, for which he needs the presence not only of his collaborator and brother Neal Jones, but also his younger partners Brian Farling and Jacob Benyi.

What we can learn is that it is entirely possible for human beings to live in the desert and to do so well and beautifully. It is true that this is a particular version of the arid landscape, one that is lusher and more expressive in its forms than many other such places. It is also true that the Phoenix area by now has a tradition of architecture that makes clients and those in charge of agreeing to and licensing buildings accepting to such forms, while there also is a tradition of machine tool workers who came to the area to work for the aerospace industry and on which architects such as Jones can draw.

Given these conditions, however, you have to be a good enough architect to realize that our place is to not replace the Sonoran Desert, nor to remove ourselves from it; not to retreat into a cave, nor to bake in the sun; not to make one move, nor to live within that statement; not to create a sense of place defined by what has been there or has been made, nor to dissolve reality; but rather to pose one's self, in balance, and to hover.

Aaron Betsky
Architect, critic, curator and writer. Dean of the School of Architecture at Taliesin, formerly the Frank Lloyd Wright School of Architecture. He was Director of the Cincinnati Art Museum from 2006 to 2014. Previously he directed the Netherlands Architecture Institute of Rotterdam. He gradated in History, the Arts and Letters in 1979 and received his master's degree in Architecture in 1983 from Yale University. He taught at Cal Poly Pomona College of Environmental Design and the University of Cincinnati. He was curator of architecture, design and digital projects at San Francisco Museum of Modern Art and curated the XI Venice Architecture Biennale in 2008. He has also worked as a designer for Frank Gehry and Hodgetts & Fung.

He has written numerous monographs on 20th-century architects, including I.M. Pei, UN Studio, Koning Eisenberg, Zaha Hadid and MVRDV. His books include Building Sex: Men, Women, Architecture and the Construction of Sexuality (William Morrow & Co, 1995), False Flat: Why Dutch Design is so Good (Phaidon, 2008) and Architecture Matters (Thames & Hudson, 2017).

Selected Projects

Jones Studio / 2016
Prairie Raptor / 2015
Singing Sands / 2012
Starwood / 2011
Outpost / 2010
Casa de Nido Osprey / 2009
Logan Collection / 2008
Scorpion / 2002
House of Five Dreams / 2001
Johnson Jones / 2000

"A timeless regional vernacular and a contemporary architectural vocabulary are intertwined in the striking work of Jones Studio. Their ability to combine these forces and instill a sense of wonder comes from a lifelong exploration of the productive tension between the durable and the delicate, and the dialogue between earth and sky. Indelible and timeless are the oases they create, offering sublime and powerful moments of respite that enrich the indelible experience of their masterful dwellings."

Marlon Blackwell

FAIA (Marlon Blackwell Architects). 2016 Smithsonian Cooper-Hewitt National Design Award. Recipient of the 2020 AIA Gold Medal.

Jones Studio

Tempe, Arizona
/ 2016

The new studio is our house and is a gesture of optimism to a forgotten, lower-income, "wrong side of the tracks" Tempe neighborhood. The investment represents a leap of faith through the creation of a beautiful example of sustainability and possibility on an infill site. We chose a small, undeveloped location in a depressed residential area near the Arizona State University campus, with its light rail stops, bike lanes, and regenerating young population. It is a 6,700 square foot masonry and glass building set in a garden irrigated with grey water and captured rain stored in a 2,500 gallon underground water harvesting tank. The building is operating at 40% below energy model predictions.

The idea was to create a simple, yet high performance building that opens to the north allowing maximum daylight to enter the studio. Between the fully glazed north facade and the car park, is a linear garden which is defined and contained by a crazy block wall in the tradition of perforated masonry screens. In contrast, the south elevation is a heavily insulated solid wall which is punctured in strategic places to cross-ventilate the interior. The custom operable casement windows surface-mounted to the inside of the wall openings are color tinted as a gift offering to the neighbors.

The interior of the studio is the epitome of a healthy work environment. The open plan layout and industrial scale pole fans augment natural ventilation, thus improving air quality and reducing the need for air conditioning. Views of nature surround the building's occupants – there's even a tree inside, marking the entrance to the restrooms. The environment is designed to inspire and stimulate the human senses – light is filtered and colored through tinted glass, reflected off brass leaves and refracted through water. Daily and seasonal rhythms are felt within the interior, and electric lighting is rarely needed during regular working hours. The "family" table provides a consistent, unifying work surface which is, nonetheless, customizable and varied to suit individual "family" members. Outreach, in the form of public lectures, tours and community meetings, occur during evening hours and weekends—giving the studio life outside the traditional nine to five.

205

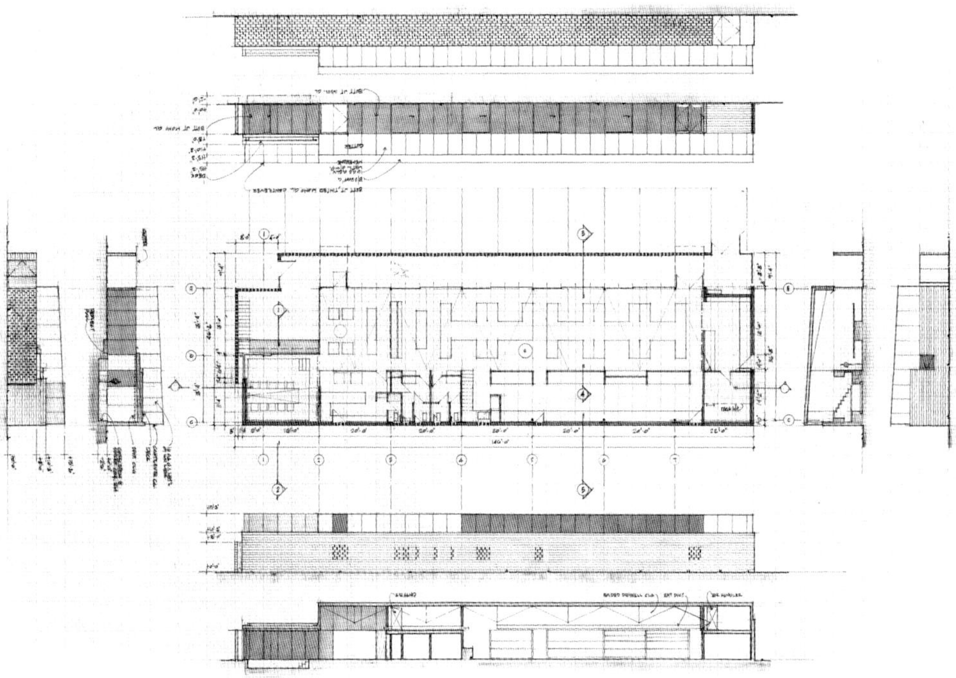

JONES STUDIO

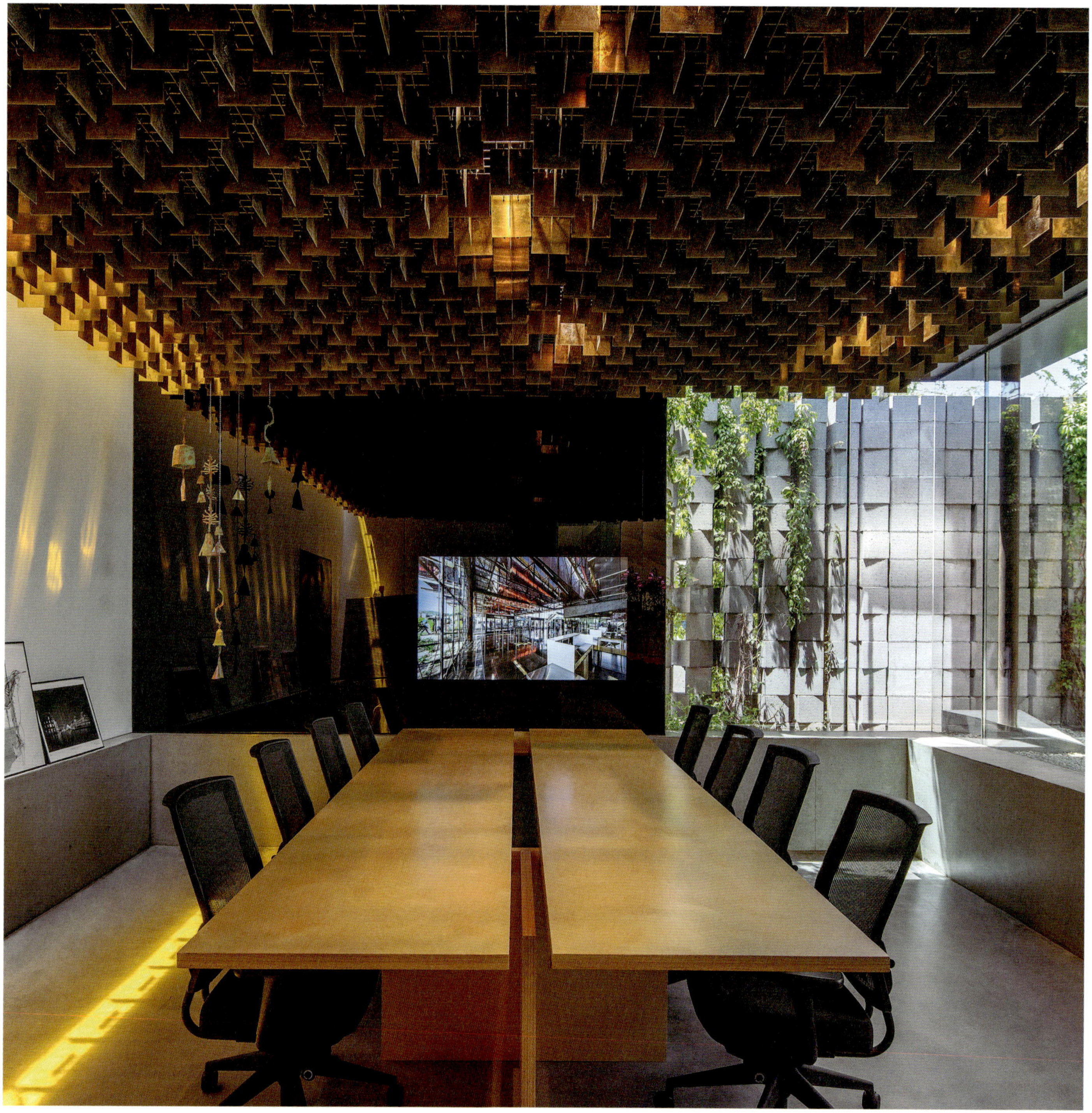

"Eddie Jones is a serious voice in a land full of flash and trendiness. He has positioned himself in the field of architecture as a potent form seeker and as a socially responsive practitioner; a combination not easily or often found."

"Eddie's work is original and uniquely responsive to material innovation and creative construction methods. They always emerge with a strong sense of place and identity because his approach to design is fundamentally about authenticity."

Lawrence Scarpa

FAIA (Brooks+Scarpa). 2014 Smithsonian Cooper-Hewitt National Design Award.
2010 National American Institute of Architects Firm of the Year.

"Eddie Jones is a first rate architect with a strong, yet sensitive personality. I appreciate his architecture which is organic in nature as it responds to client needs, site, structure, use of materials, forms and mass. Eddie is also an eloquent writer and a friend. I give Eddie my finest appreciation and regard for his work and person."

Herb Greene

Architect, Artist, Author.

Prairie Raptor

Oklahoma City, Oklahoma
/ 2015

Unknown to the most recent generation of architects, a strange but wonderful house still "lives" outside Norman, Oklahoma, quietly at home with the vast horizon and prairie grasses. Built in 1954, it was the great architect Herb Greene's first completed project. Locals have always called it the "Prairie Chicken." I first saw it as a college student and its image of frozen poetry never left me.

"Prairie Raptor" does not aim at "Prairie Chicken" 20 miles to the south, rather its crosshairs are centered on the tallest structure in Oklahoma City: a skyscraper for BIG OIL!

Sited in the middle of forty heavily wooded acres, the architecture is intended to eventually merge with the color and texture of the bare winter trees surrounding it. There is one large sheltering wood roof, shingled with two-by-twelve boards lapped like the feathers on a giant predator bird. Over time, the creature will age, turn silver-gray and twist, alongside the winter trees shedding their foliage.

Denser, smaller feathers cover the body as deep black bricks. The manganese additive gives the walls an iridescent blue shimmer in direct light similar to an expensive tuxedo. Thin, custom steel and glass wall framing adds the elegant persimmon pinstripe.

Who lives here?

The African serval cat is a 40-plus pound feline; speedy and graceful with very long, sharp teeth. There are three of them sharing occupancy with the owners. Human visitors enter and move cautiously through the cats' jungle. A transparent loft provides an ideal elevated, defensible position for Simba, Nala and Samson to observe the entering fresh meat!

Strips of clear pharmaceutical vials ring the skylight momentarily transforming the sun into crystal clear bubbles of light.

Barn

The architecture is not a wounded bird; it is not the "Prairie Chicken." It represents the speed, grace and aggression of a fully alive wildness eager to return to nature.

The sooner, the better!

The Barn

Maintaining forty acres of heavily wooded Oklahoma landscape requires a rather large collection of equipment. During summer months, the owner enjoys a meditative state of consciousness as he maneuvers the riding lawn mower for hours... his only responsibility being the avoidance of trees.

The quarter-mile gravel road disappears under winter snow. Less so, during these times of climatic change. Snow removal requires a different kind of tractor rigging and takes up additional storage space.

However, it is the five beautiful horses the neighbor gifted that depend on the most area for storing feed, tack and riding gear.

Frankly, I was more than happy to add a barn to the overall raptor design ensemble and was relieved it was actually necessary!

Perhaps in another year or two we can start on the running paths, fish pond and the construction of a romantic picnic gazebo cantilevered over the water.

Previous spread, above and below Title: Job 3278: Herb Greene, Greene House (Norman, Oklahoma). Author/Creator: Julius Shulman, photographer. Creation Date: 1961. Credit: © J. Paul Getty Trust. Getty Research Institute, Los Angeles (2004.R.10).

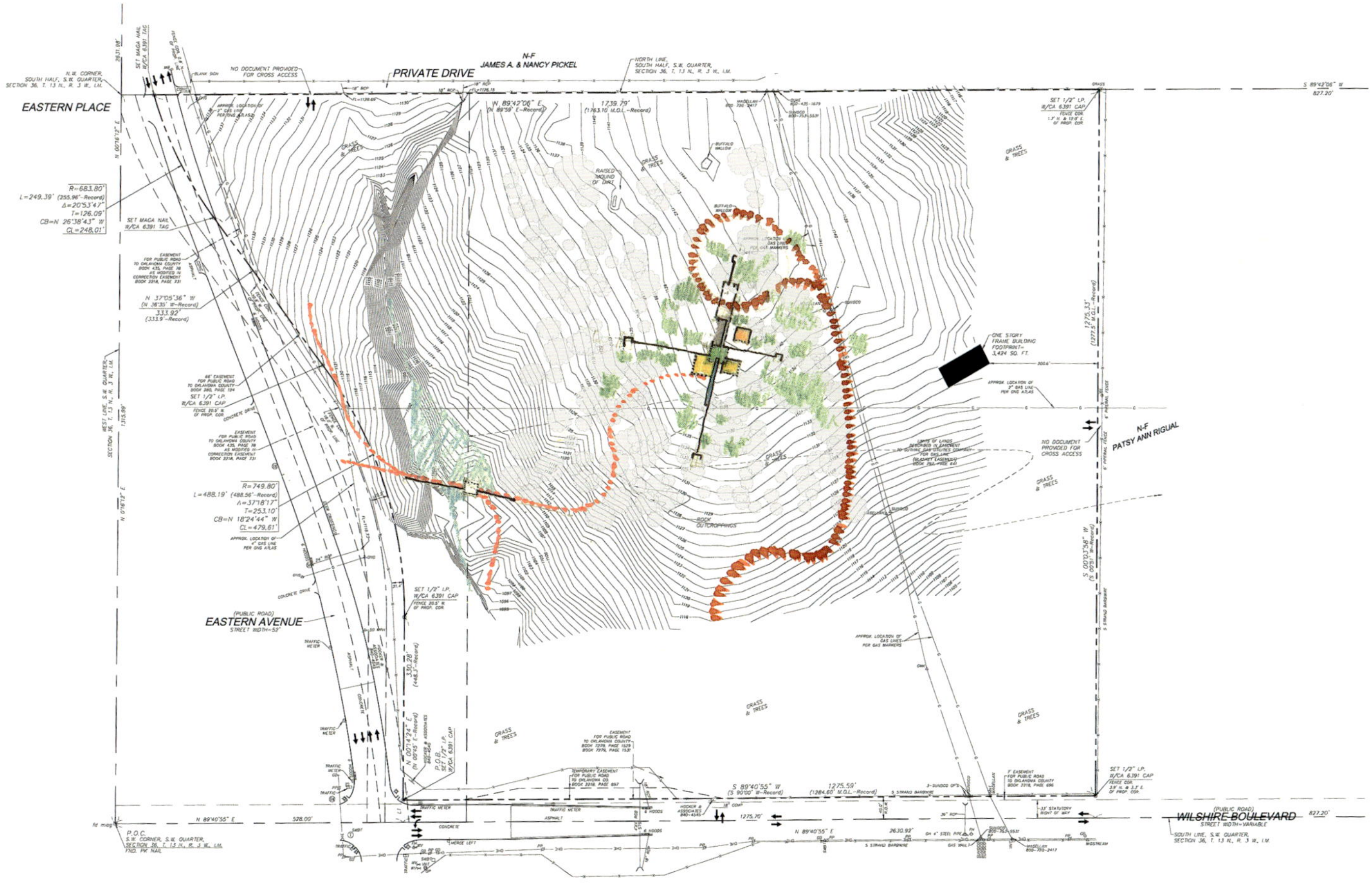
N-F
JAMES A. & NANCY PICKEL
PRIVATE DRIVE
EASTERN PLACE
EASTERN AVENUE
(PUBLIC ROAD)
WILSHIRE BOULEVARD
N-F
PATSY ANN RIGUAL
ONE STORY
FRAME BUILDING
FOOTPRINT=
3,424 SQ. FT.
NO DOCUMENT PROVIDED FOR CROSS ACCESS
GRASS & TREES
ROCK OUTCROPPINGS

prairie raptor · johnson house

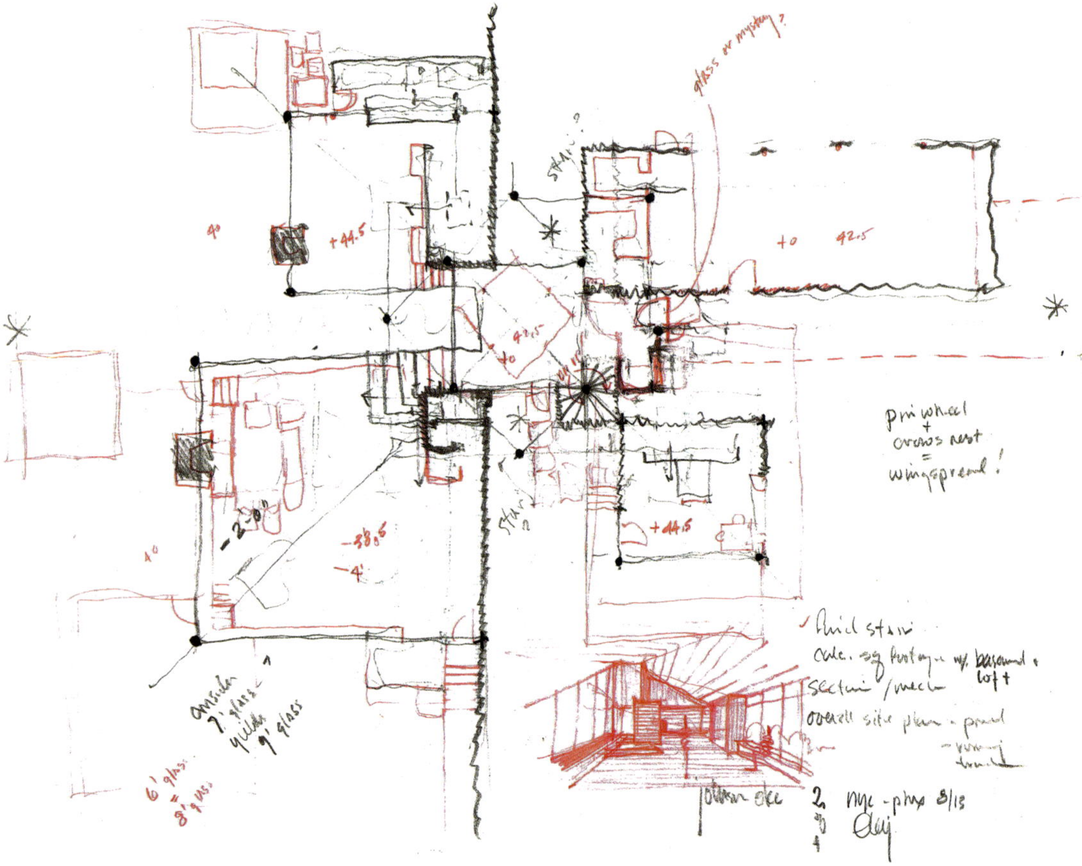
+44.5
+0
42.5
+44.5
-4'
pinwheel
+
crows nest
=
wingspread!

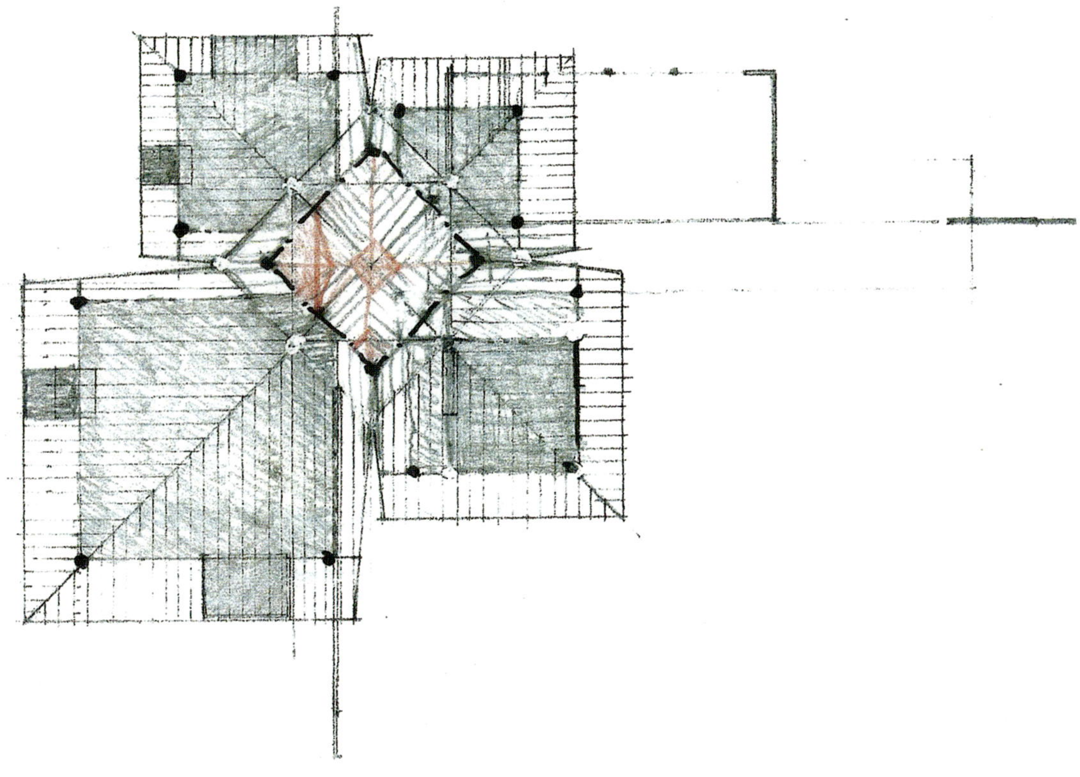

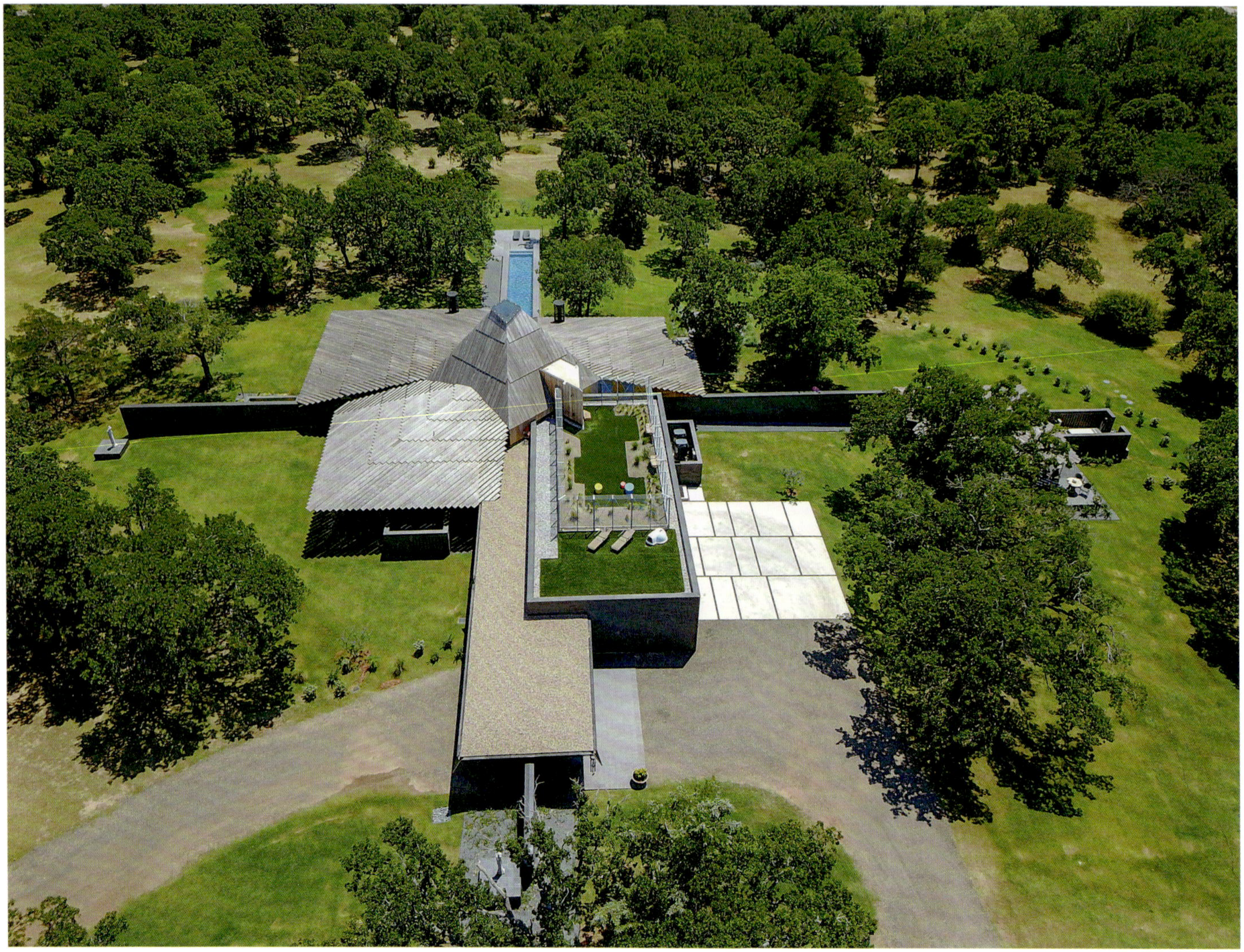

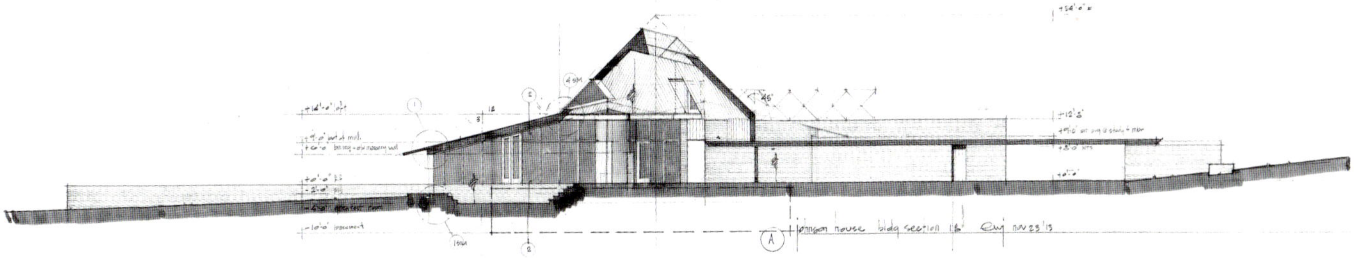

tamp - charl - phx 9/13 Sept 11

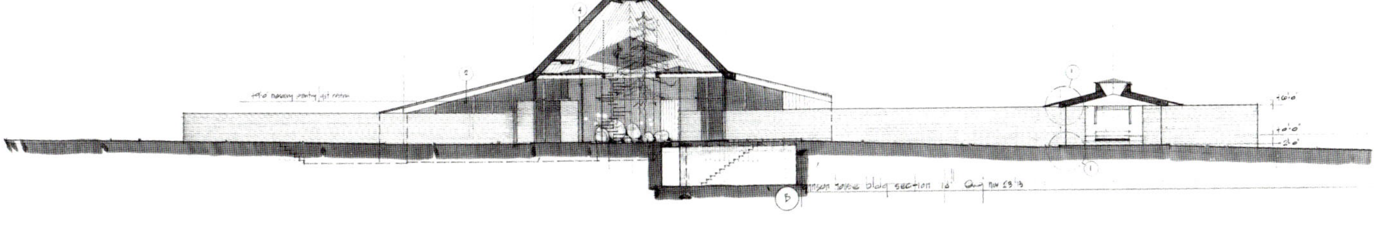

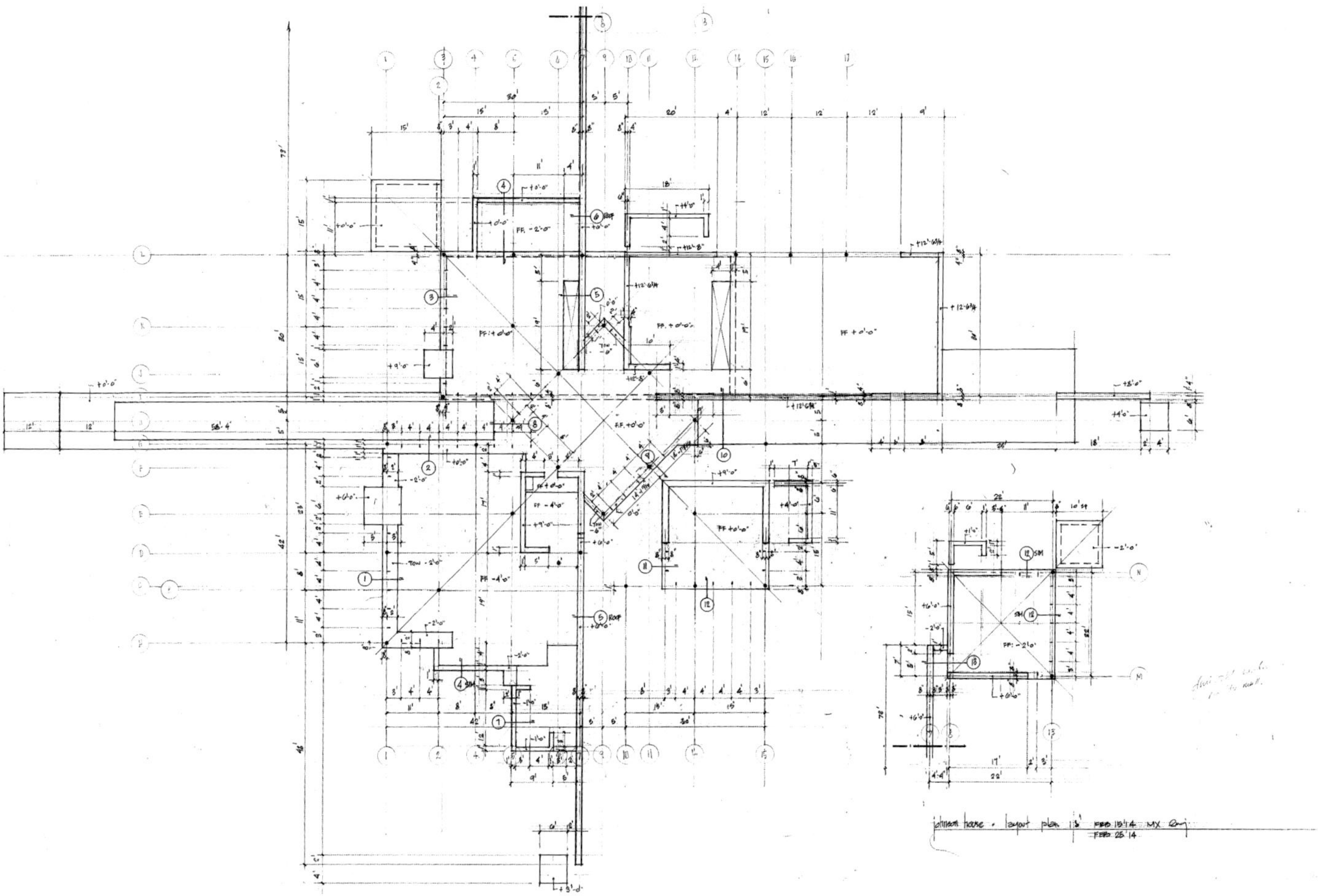
johnson house · layout plan 1/8" FEB 15'14 MX
FEB 25'14

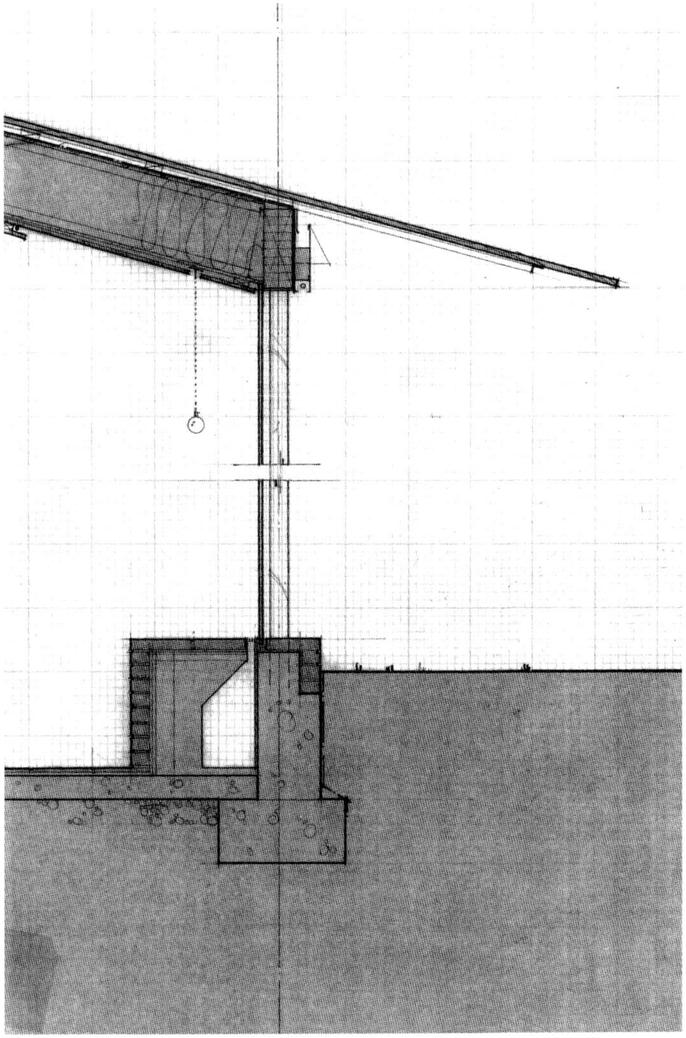

“The work of Eddie Jones is both irrepressible and disciplined. When his beautiful forms take flight, they are held aloft by rigor.”

Billie Tsien

AIA (Tod Williams Billie Tsien Architects). 2013 National American Institute of Architects Firm of the Year. 2003 Smithsonian Cooper-Hewitt National Design Award.

Singing Sands

Canon Beach, Oregon
/ 2016

"Cottages are idealized as retreats for pursing familial pleasures, artistic creativity, fairy tales, and enhanced appreciation for natural surroundings."

Cannon Beach Cottages
Jill Grady, 2005

The first recorded non-Indian homestead within the Cannon Beach area is dated 1848, followed by the Brooklyn Camp development, late 1800s, and the Presidential Streets recorded in 1903. As each new generation discovered the secrets of the Oregon coast, cottage architecture evolved in size, shape and materiality. Nevertheless, one can trace vernacular elements of construction incorporating local building materials such as sea shells, driftwood and glass floats which, in other American locations, may not be socially acceptable.

The Oregon State Historic Preservation office loosely defines cottage classic features to include wood frame construction, gable roofs, overhanging eaves with exposed rafter ends, wood shingles/siding and wood double hung or casement windows. These design elements have become representative of our feelings of stability, freedom, authenticity, sharing and nurturing "family."

Although classic, these same elements in new construction tend to utilize the benefits of new technologies and can appear to project a more modern construction aesthetic.

It would seem the single most defining characteristic to have endured historic cottage design evolution would be, for today… scale! The Basha Family is large! However, to Eddie and Nadine's credit, there has been a consistent commitment to sacrifice maximum allowable square footage in exchange for scale and intimacy.

Lot six, Arcadia Beach, has a unique building envelope! Placement of the main structure is shaped as an "L" with a detached additional envelope for a two car garage. This split had a positive design influence and resulted in an opportunity to introduce a beautiful private outdoor room formed by a circular circulation pattern. The curved form of the garden side is an appropriate organic geometry reinforcing the foreground character of the "contained" natural flower space. In contrast, the ocean side has a classically composed transparent wall parallel to the dynamic, vast panoramic view.

It is worth noting, along with the covered outdoor entry path, we have outdoor access to the two guest rooms, eliminating additional square footage usually required for interior hallways.

In addition to the three bedrooms, there is a small "crow's nest" loft elevated, yet integrated into the dominant main gable roof. This is the retreat... a space removed for quiet contemplation, reading and painting.

Existing topography and envelope locations dictated a structural retaining wall built into the northeast slope. The design intent was to use an old-fashioned method of forming concrete with vertical wood boards allowing the grain and joint pattern to emboss permanently into the finished product. Other walls with lateral structural requirements utilize this same material, and are balanced with vertical wood siding at the structurally non-lateral areas.

Sustainable architecture has, fortunately, become mainstream. For the Basha family, responsible environmental design has always been an enduring ethic. The Arcadia Beach cottage promises to be an outstanding example of rainwater collection and management, minimal energy consumption, certified sustainable material use, and perhaps most importantly, a new home expressing profound respect for a beautiful old site, the historic seaside community, and new neighbors.

"entry" 6/09

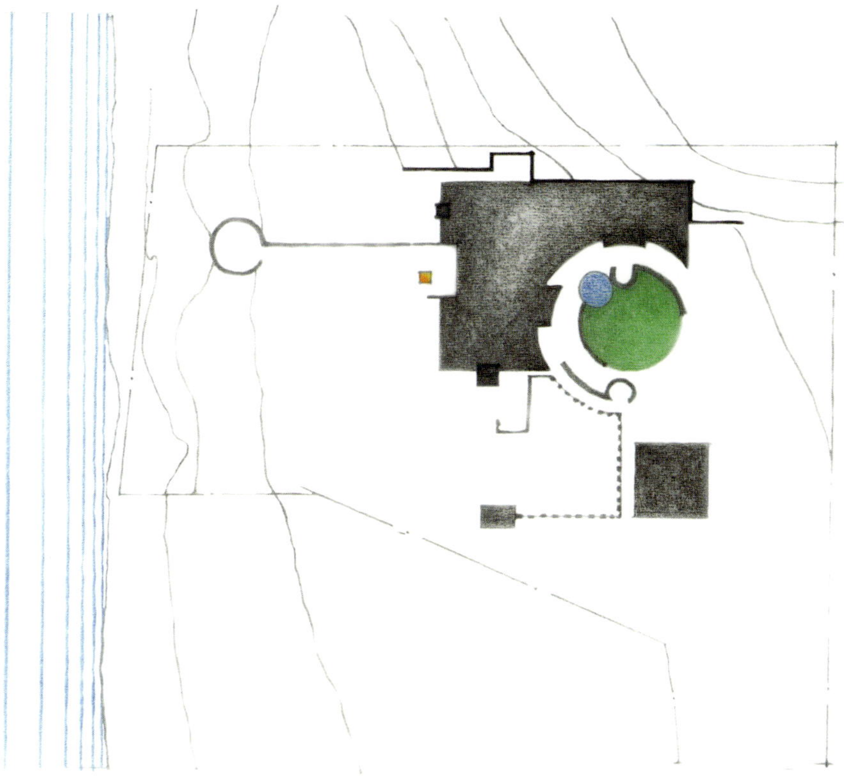

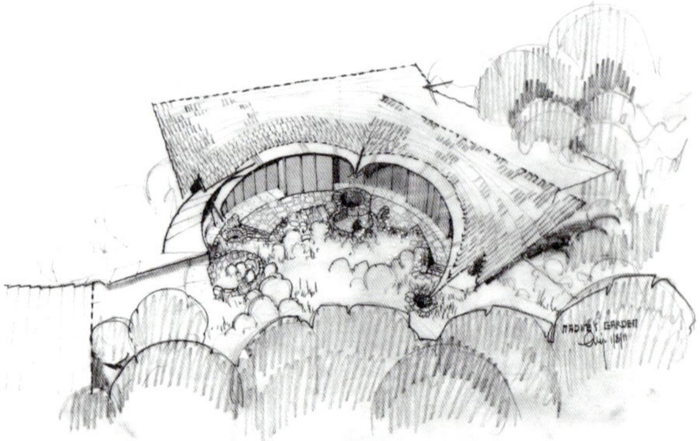

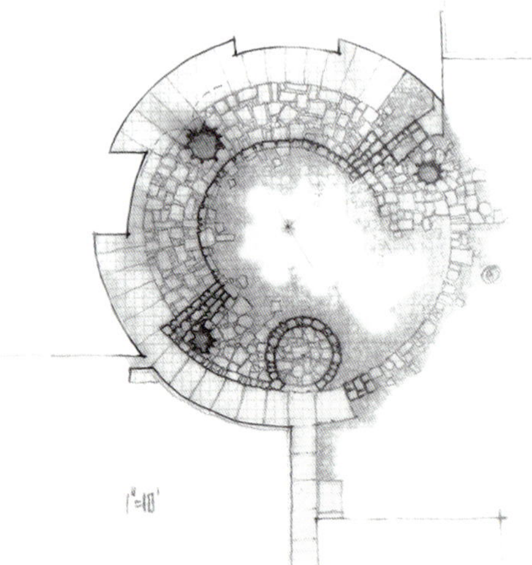

basha cottage, cannon beach, or.

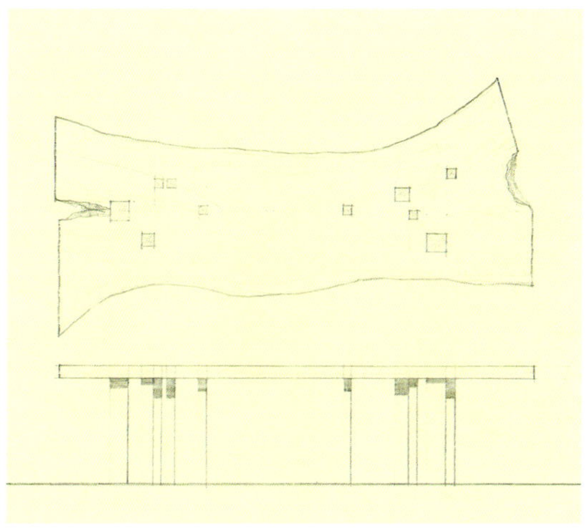

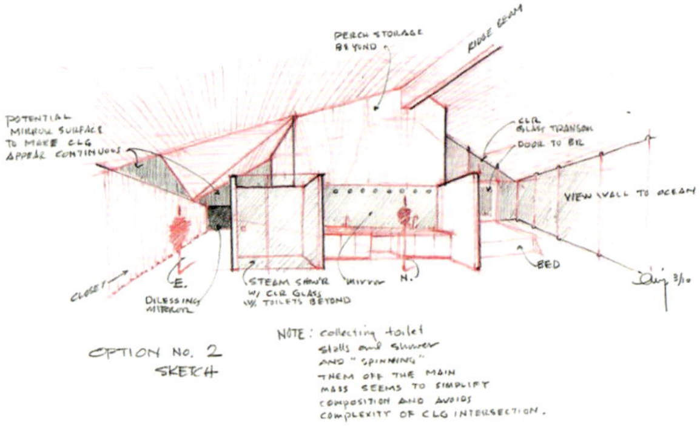
PERCH STORAGE BEYOND
RIDGE BEAM
POTENTIAL MIRROR SURFACE TO MAKE CLG APPEAR CONTINUOUS
CLR GLASS TRANSOM
DOOR TO BR
VIEW WALL TO OCEAN
CLOSET
E.
DRESSING MIRROR
STEAM SHOW'R W/ CLR GLASS W/ TOILETS BEYOND
MIRROR
N.
BED
3/10
OPTION NO. 2 SKETCH
NOTE: collecting toilet stalls and shower AND "SPINNING" THEM OFF THE MAIN MASS SEEMS TO SIMPLIFY COMPOSITION AND AVOIDS COMPLEXITY OF CLG INTERSECTION.

113

"*Granpa, you drew a farm*", Gibson Jones - 3 years old

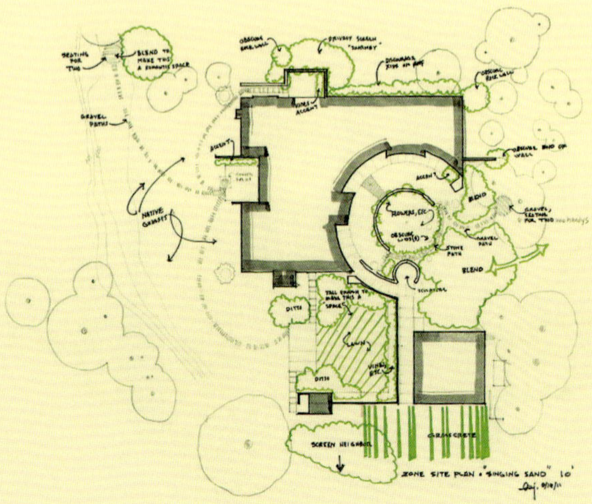

“Eddie and Jones Studio’s work always exudes joy, surprise and a love of craft and making things well with a broad range of materials across every project scale. Most importantly no space, no small decision is ever mundane but in fact the very thing that makes each project a sheer delight to experience as a total work of architecture.”

Wendell Burnette

FAIA (Wendell Burnette Architects). 1999 Emerging Voices Award, Architectural League of New York.

Starwood

Missoula, Montana
/ 2011

As architects, we hope the result of our collaborative effort qualifies as architecture. Sometimes we are graced with the good fortune of exceptional craftsmanship, which yields a building quality proudly described as "furniture." Then, there are those extremely rare projects where the owner, contractor, subcontractor, and architect come together in a spirit beyond their individual visions and soar to a level of built excellence, which can only be described as a "jewel box."

It began as a simple two-thousand square foot addition. The new living/dining/kitchen pavilion respected the square pyramidal roof of the existing house, but introduced a material departure. Later, a new detached garage was added, extending the composition of pitched forms. It became necessary for the original home to "catch up." With the existing structure remaining intact, a new program, materials, and glazing details elevated the original form to the larger collection of louvered architecture. The small addition evolved into a three-building composition. Responding to the existing residence and site amenities, the location of the two new buildings respected native wildlife habitats and preserved natural vegetation.

During the winter, the giant stainless steel shingles of the living room roof befriend the whiteness of snow while its perforated geometric edge encourages a veil of icicles. Subordinate buildings are clad in beautiful raw steel, rusted for several days face down on a "casting bed" of damp grass before installation.

125

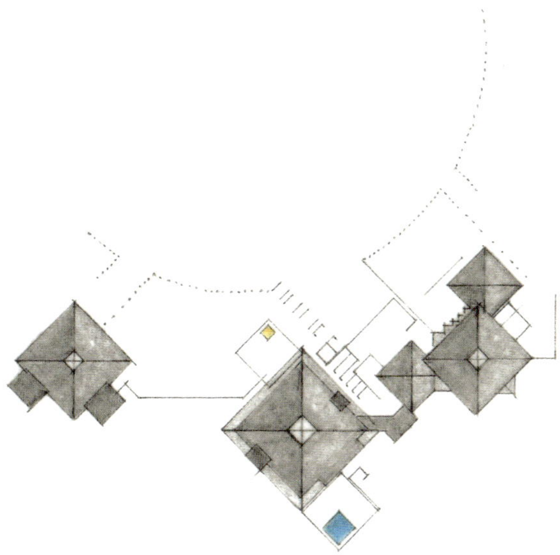

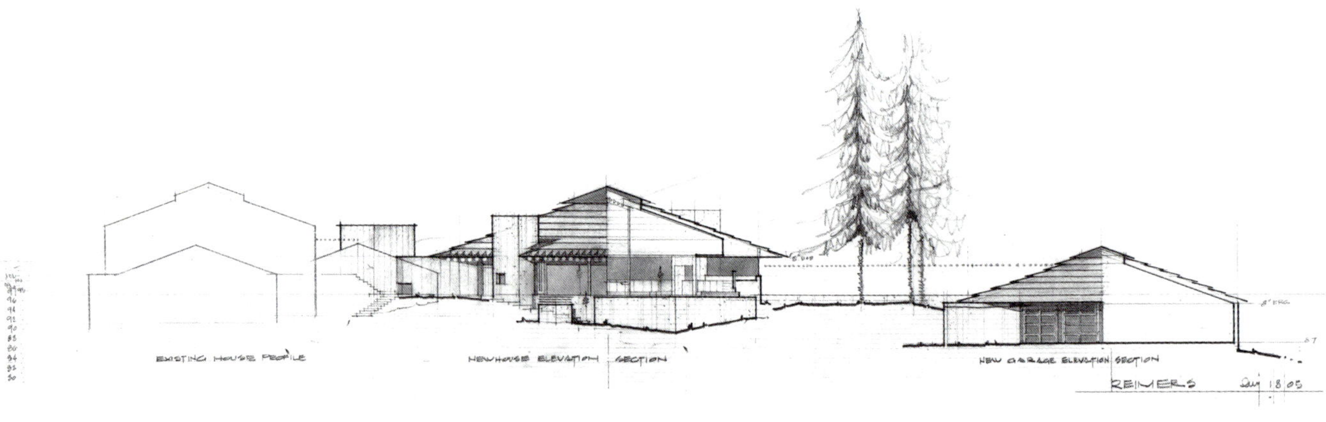
EXISTING HOUSE PROFILE
NEWHOUSE ELEVATION SECTION
NEW GARAGE ELEVATION SECTION
REIMERS

129

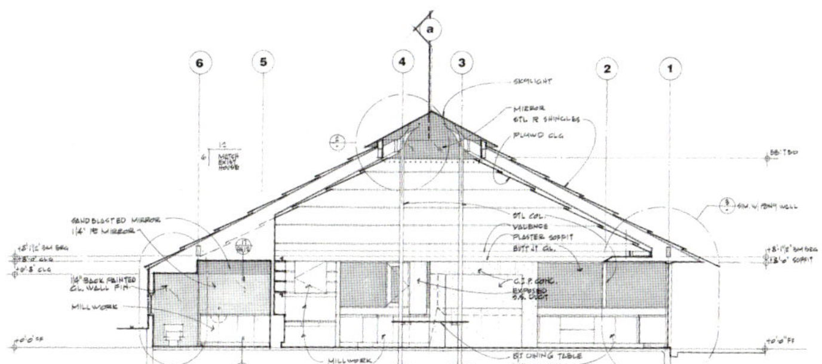

SECTION CC ¼" = 1'-0"

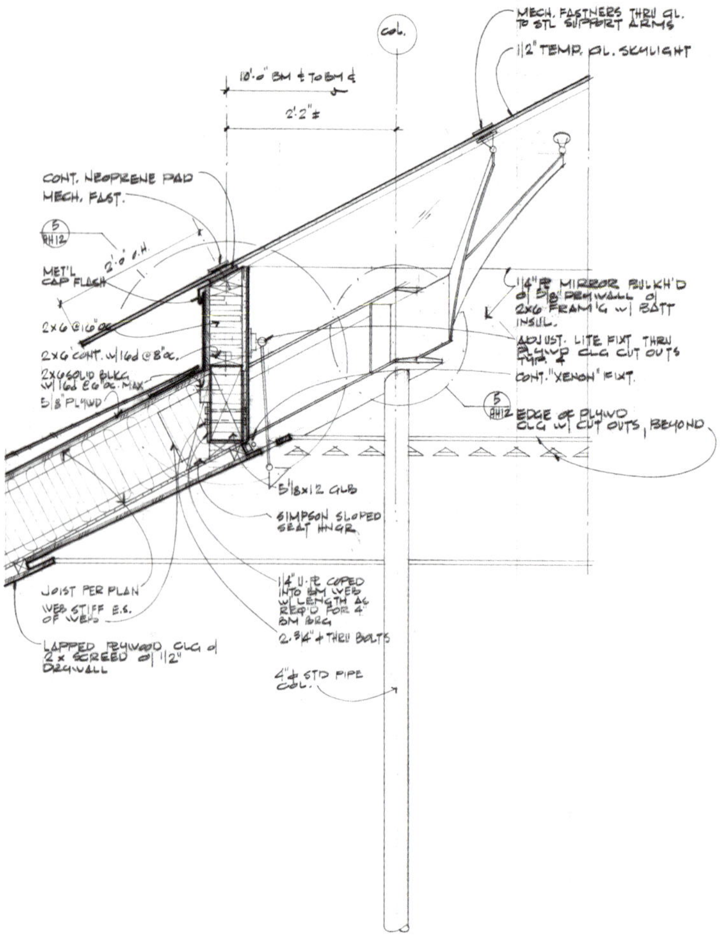
MECH. FASTNERS THRU GL. TO STL SUPPORT ARMS
1/2" TEMP. GL. SKYLIGHT
COL.
10'-0" BM ℄ TO BM ℄
2'-2" ±
CONT. NEOPRENE PAD
MECH. FAST.
5
AH12
2'-0" O.H.
MET'L CAP FLASH
2x6 @16" oc
2x6 CONT. w/ 16d @ 8" oc.
2x6 SOLID BLKG w/ 16d @ 6" oc. MAX
5/8" PLYWD
1/4" ℞ MIRROR BULKH'D o/ 5/8" PLYWALL o/ 2x6 FRAM'G w/ BATT INSUL.
ADJUST. LITE FIXT THRU PLYWD CLG CUT OUTS TYP. 4
CONT. "XENON" FIXT.
EDGE OF PLYWD CLG w/ CUT OUTS, BEYOND
5 1/8 x 12 GLB
SIMPSON SLOPED SEAT HNGR
JOIST PER PLAN
WEB STIFF E.S. OF WEB
1/4" U-℞ COPED INTO BM WEB w/ LENGTH AS REQ'D FOR 4" BM BRG
2-3/4" ⌀ THRU BOLTS
LAPPED PLYWOOD CLG o/ 2x SCREED o/ 1/2" DRYWALL
4" ⌀ STD PIPE COL.

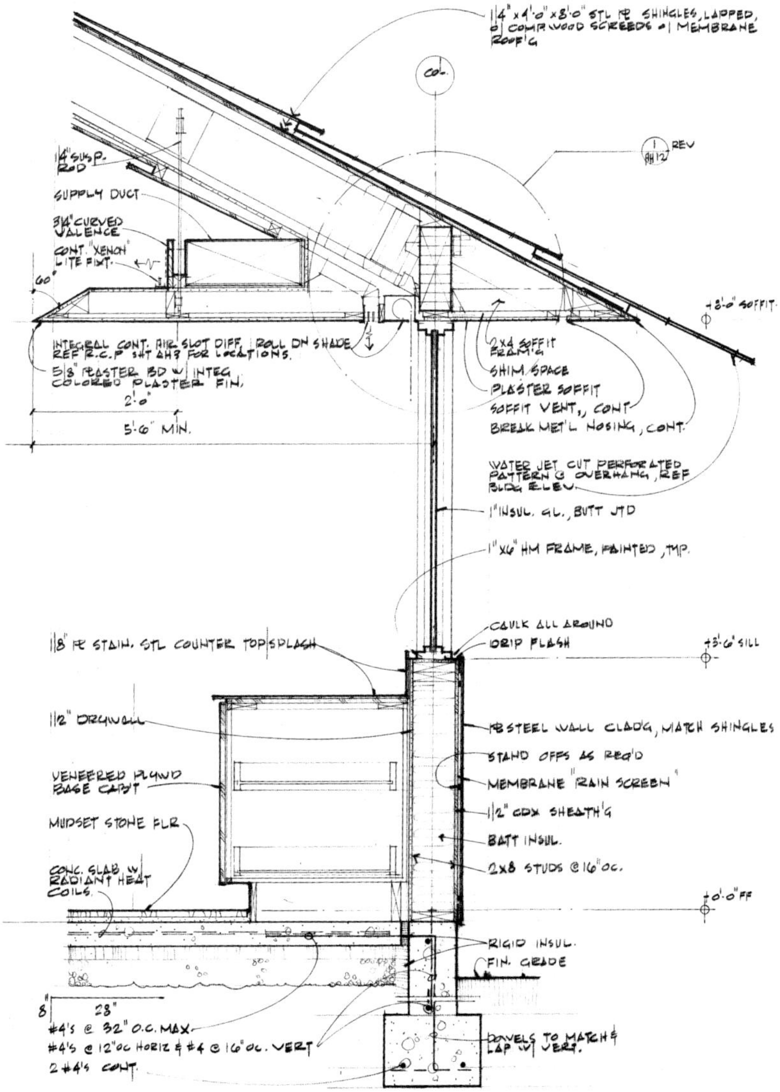
1/4" x 4'-0" x 8'-0" STL PL SHINGLES, LAPPED, o/ COMP. WOOD SCREEDS o/ MEMBRANE ROOF'G
CO.
1 AH12 REV
1/4" SUSP. ROD
SUPPLY DUCT
3/4" CURVED VALENCE
CONT. "XENON" LITE FIXT.
60°
+8'-0" SOFFIT
INTEGRAL CONT. AIR SLOT DIFF. ROLL ON SHADE REF R.C.P SHT AH3 FOR LOCATIONS.
5/8" PLASTER BD w/ INTEG COLORED PLASTER FIN.
2'-0"
5'-6" MIN.
2x4 SOFFIT FRAM'G
SHIM SPACE
PLASTER SOFFIT
SOFFIT VENT, CONT
BREAK MET'L NOSING, CONT.
WATER JET CUT PERFORATED PATTERN @ OVERHANG, REF BLDG ELEV.
1" INSUL. GL., BUTT JTD
1" x 6" HM FRAME, PAINTED, TYP.
CAULK ALL AROUND
DRIP FLASH
+3'-6" SILL
1/8" PL STAIN. STL COUNTER TOP/SPLASH
1/2" DRYWALL
PL STEEL WALL CLAD'G, MATCH SHINGLES
STAND OFFS AS REQ'D
VENEERED PLYWD BASE CAB'T
MEMBRANE "RAIN SCREEN"
1/2" CDX SHEATH'G
MUDSET STONE FLR
BATT INSUL.
2x8 STUDS @ 16" oc.
CONC. SLAB w/ RADIANT HEAT COILS.
+0'-0" FF
RIGID INSUL.
FIN. GRADE
8"
28"
#4's @ 32" O.C. MAX.
#4's @ 12" oc HORIZ & #4 @ 16" oc. VERT
2 #4's CONT.
DOWELS TO MATCH & LAP w/ VERT.

135

"I believe Eddie to be, without a doubt, one of the most inspired Architects in the American West. He is a highly skilled communicator of his humanist beliefs and critically regional architectural observances and has the tools to help us all bring our souls and intellects into alignment."

Rick Joy

FAIA, Int. FRIBA (Studio Rick Joy). 2015 College of Fellows, Royal Institute of British Architects. 2004 Smithsonian Cooper-Hewitt National Design Award.

Outpost

Paradise Valley, Arizona
/ 2010

There's no such thing as an ordinary day where I work. Even by Jones Studio standards, May 6th, 2009 was exceptional. Although I knew he was talking with other architects (the usual suspects), I was not expecting a call from the infamous "Lacey."

Most people know Michael Lacey by reputation. As I did, we assume his hard-hitting, "take no prisoners" personality would make a relationship challenging.

It did, and it does, but I love the guy.

So I take the call. Because, regardless of his intimidating image, I enjoy interesting people. He takes me to the property where he intends to build his new home. I was not yet aware specific preparation for this commission had started decades in advance.

September, 1966, Michael Lacey enrolls in Arizona State University. Although quite intelligent, he is not a good student—something about incompatibility with mandatory attendance. He drops out.

In response to the 1970 Kent State shootings, Lacey, with several other anti-war activists, starts the Valley's first counterculture newspaper: *New Times*. Without fear of consequence, he takes on corruption; he takes on giants, including Charles Keating, the Keating responsible for the 1989 collapse of Lincoln Savings and Loan.[1]

Above left Title: "In the Nature of Materials: The Buildings of Frank Lloyd Wright 1887-1941". Author/Creator: Henry Russell Hitchcock, author. Publication Date: 1942. Publisher: Da Capo Press, Inc. (subsidiary of Plenum Publishing Corporation). ISBN: 0-306-80019-5. Book with frayed edges and faded print.

Above right Title: "In the Nature of Materials: The Buildings of Frank Lloyd Wright 1887-1941". Author/Creator: Henry Russell Hitchcock, author. Publication Date: 1942. Publisher: Da Capo Press, Inc. (subsidiary of Plenum Publishing Corporation). ISBN: 0-306-80019-5. Photograph of Miss Paulson's living room through the two story glass wall.

Due in part to Lacey's investigative reporting, Keating goes to jail, and his large track of Paradise Valley property located on the southeast corner of Lincoln and 32nd Street sells and is subdivided.

Now, retired from the newspaper business, Lacey buys a lot on the old Keating property with the highest elevation. The one that looks down on all the rest.

There we are, standing on the property, enjoying mountain views and knowing the potential for sunsets and city lights. However, I am mentally distracted by the blurry memories that begin to detach somewhere from the bottom of my mind.

That evening in my library, I easily find in *The Nature of Materials.*[2] This is my very first architecture book, now resting in the company of two thousand more. I bought it in 1964 with paper route savings. The edges are frayed, the print is a little faded, but overall, still in good condition, much like its owner. My memory takes me to a particular page with a photograph taken inside Miss Pauson's living room looking north through a two-story glass wall. Just as I remembered, in this window, I could see it. There was a hill: Lacey's hill!

Above left and right Title: "Building the Pauson House: The Letters of Frank Lloyd Wright and Rose Pauson". Author/Creator: Allan Wright Green, author. Publication Date: 2011. Publisher: Pomegranate Communications, Inc. ISBN: 978-0-7649-5888-5.

1940 was the year Frank Lloyd Wright completed construction on his first Arizona residential commission, breaking his self-imposed rule to never build on top of a hill. The Rose Pauson house was accidentally destroyed by fire six months after the Pauson Sisters moved in. I moved to Arizona in August 1973. I visited the then 32-year-old burnt out Pauson ruins now dubbed "Shiprock" by the locals. The unique and powerful entry sequence could still be understood and its influence sunk into my subconscious: a young architect, not yet licensed, eager to explore forces of nature and lessons from those who had lived before.

Shiprock, I presume, was a name based on a description of stone foundations riding the crest of a hill like a ship rides cresting water. The longer the structure, the more accent there is on the curvature of the slope, the height of a breaking wave. Hold the top of the wall level while the bottom of the wall drops with the falling contours, and the contrast will define the shape of the knoll.

The topographic similarities between the Lacey and Shiprock sites were obvious. Could it have been predestined that Lacey's house would straddle its hilltop as well? No, too pretentious. However, precedence and memory give substance to critical design decisions, and I liked the story that had begun to develop.

I enthusiastically shared these thoughts with Lacey. Great idea to symbolically tie his hill to the Pauson Hill, his architecture to a Phoenix landmark long gone, and nod to an American hero: Frank Lloyd Wright.

That was a mistake!

Who knew Lacey placed Wright's social conduct down there with Keating's hypocrisy! I made sure there would be no more verbalized FLLW references, but the ideas were solid and I continued.

The Lacey walls elongate dramatically in three directions accentuating the profile of the ground plane. Fortunately, the program included a modern lap pool. I used this major linear element as a permission slip to complete the third topographic axis, finding directional purpose in its exact center alignment with the six million year old Papago Peak six miles to the south.

Any conceptual similarities to a forgotten ruin are coincidental!

Recalling the memory of an inspired Hilltop approach, a Lacey visitor arrives at the bottom of the hill, assumes the entry is somewhere up there, and ascends masonry ledges melted into the slope, the entry sequence eventually topping out in a space surrounded by separated buildings; a composition of striated dirt walls, weather-twisted wood and a fully encroaching Sonoran landscape. For centuries, the unique qualities of southwest lifestyle have confirmed the precedent of living spaces arranged around a courtyard. It is the void or left over space between buildings that organize the traditional Spanish hacienda.

Above left & right Title: "Building the Pauson House: The Letters of Frank Lloyd Wright and Rose Pauson". Author/Creator: Allan Wright Green, author. Publication Date: 2011. Publisher: Pomegranate Communications, Inc. ISBN: 978-0-7649-5888-5

Andy Goldsworthy is an artist favored by many people, including myself.[3] The spiritually youthful Englishman has an enviable ability to give nature voice using natural materials as if they were his own vocabulary. In his book, simply but provocatively titled *Time*,[4] He reminds me that, in spite of my best efforts, nature will always repossess my buildings. Without mercy, without question, she is continuously reclaiming her materials and taking back her land, the land we foolishly think we own. I have learned to embrace this inevitability, to honor it, and admit that nature, in the process of reclamation, is a much better designer of shape, color, and pattern than I can ever be.

When I was in college, I never related architecture to art. Now, older and more inclusive, I lecture to college students, typically using two Goldsworthy examples to demonstrate a spectrum of time-related outcomes regarding structure. The first example is an intricately woven nest of tiny twigs gathered quickly and locally. Left behind, it is eliminated within the weeks of a passing season without indicating it was ever there. Whether consumed by an accidental fire or deconstructed by weather, wood transitions quickly.

The second Goldsworthy example is a series of arches constructed during low tide. Although made of durable stone, the structure is taken out in one, eight-hour tidal movement. Despite the disappearance of his work, Goldsworthy's efforts leave a mark. This is the ruin, the "Shiprock."

Lacey's house is part of the same natural poetry. It will only be finished when it is gone. Until then, each year, it becomes less about construction and more about materials in natural transition. The colors, shapes, and patterns attributed to my hand are slowly and surely being redrawn by those forces of nature I was so eager to explore long ago.

Above Title: "Time". Author/Creator: Andy Goldsworthy, photographer. Photo Date: April-August 1999. Publication Date: 2000. Publisher: Harry N. Abrams, Inc. ISBN: 0-8109-4482-0

Above Title: "Time". Author/Creator: Andy Goldsworthy, photographer. Photo Date: October 17, 1995. Publication Date: 2000. Publisher: Harry N. Abrams, Inc.. ISBN: 0-8109-4482-0

Rammed earth construction has a 1000-year history in the desert southwest. Although ancient, its resistance to climatic beatings, its compressive strength, superior insulation, and an undeniable beauty secures its relevance into the twenty-first century. Rammed earth is the timeless stone of the Goldsworthy example. Sheer weight and mass convincingly connect Lacey's architecture to its site as if the massive walls erupted from the ground up, a result of some great seismic shift. In a thousand more years, Lacey's dirt walls will still be transforming and they will leave their mark.
In contrast to the longevity of dirt, there is the fragility of Lacey's other material. It is crazy to use wood in the desert. In one summer, this searing heat will significantly alter its character. The color moves from ochre to silver-gray. The straight edge gives way to compound twisting as the wood fibers react to fluctuating expansion and contraction. Constricting surfaces relax in cracks. Veins of black trace the chemical reactions of wet/dry cycles.

1 When Lincoln Savings failed, it cost the federal government over $3 billion dollars and twenty-three thousand customers, including a house client of mine, were left with worthless bonds. In the early 1990s, Keating was convicted in both State and Federal courts on fraud, racketeering and conspiracy.
2 Henry Russell Hitchcock, In the Nature of Materials, 1887 to 1941: The Buildings of Frank Lloyd Wright (New York: Da Capo Press, 1942).
3 Andy Goldsworthy was born in Cheshire, England in 1956 and currently resides in Scotland. He has been making art in the environment, both rural and urban, since the mid-seventies. He works with natural materials that often originate from the local site.
4 Andy Goldsworthy and Terry Friedman, Time (New York: Abrams, 2008).

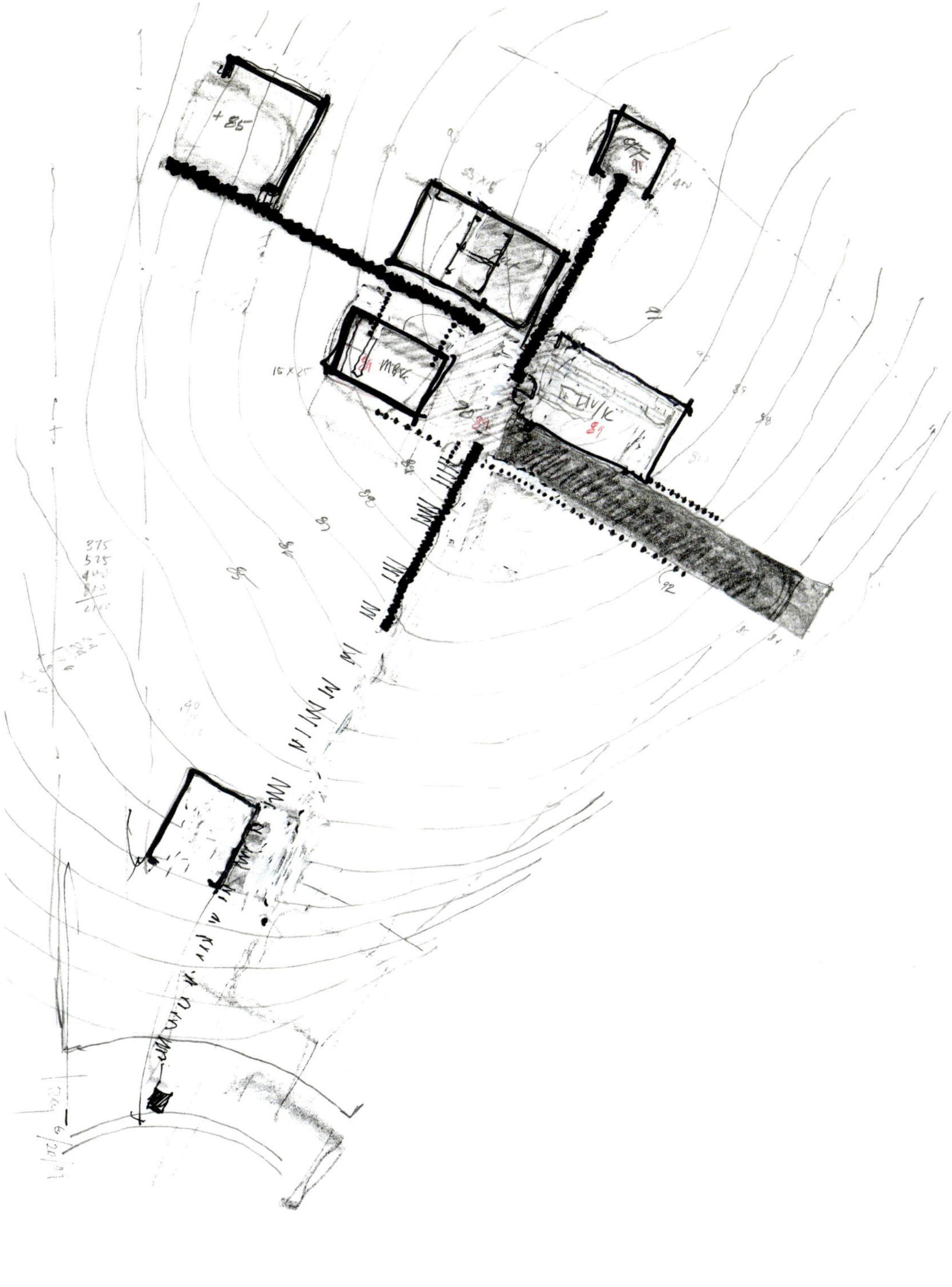

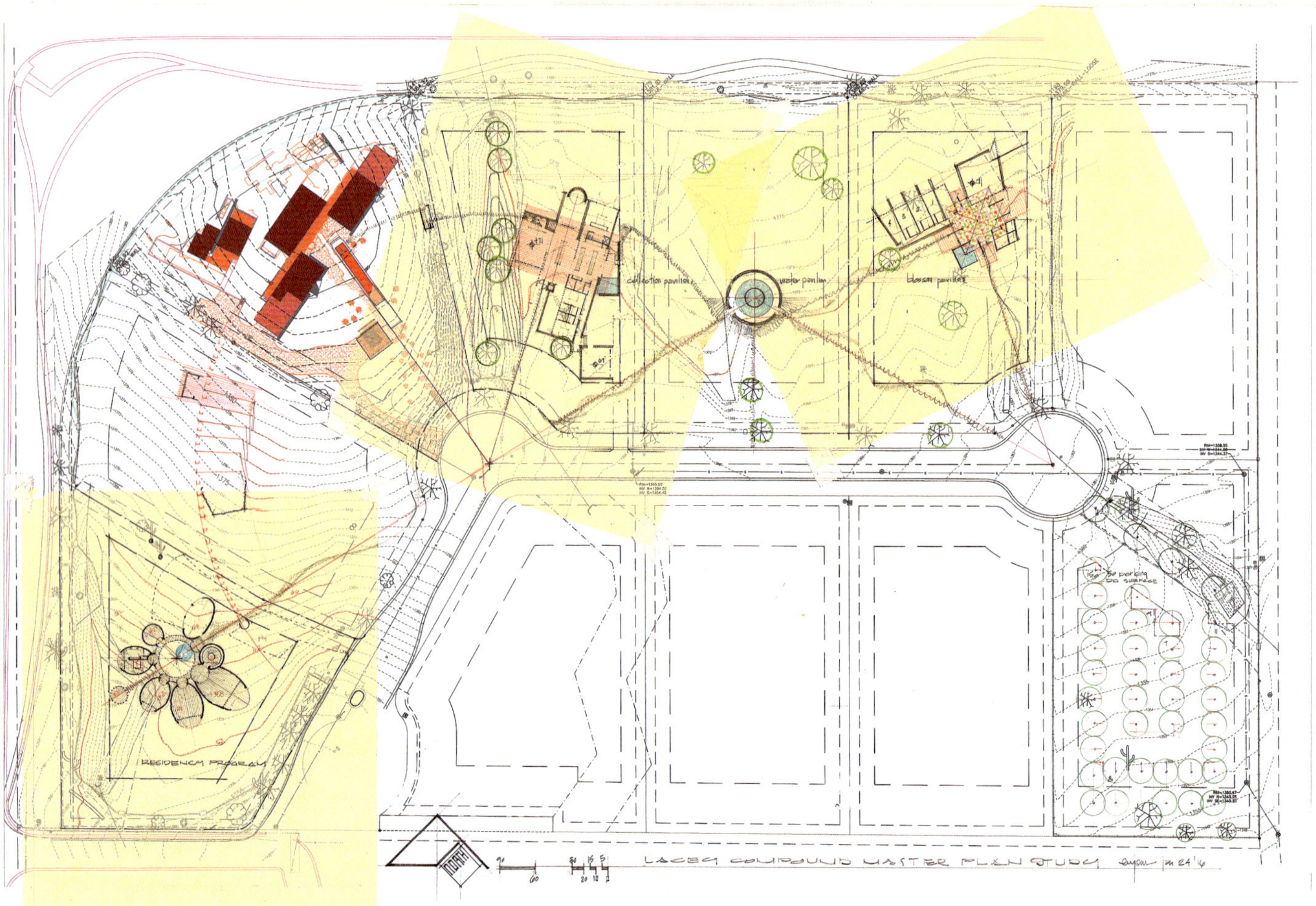
collection pavilion
water pavilion
blossom pavilion
RESIDENCY PROGRAM
NORTH
LACEY COMPOUND MASTER PLAN STUDY

Lacey... tough guy, fearless reporter, newspaper mogul, made a life inviting confrontation.

“H O L D F A S T” is tattooed on his knuckles! Really, it is.

Yet, respite, peace, safe haven, and home was his implied program for a residence meant to represent progressive thinking grounded in the fundamentals of, in his words, “mud and shadow.”

Clearly, Lacey’s home design started a long time ago. An early fascination with the nature of materials, a stone ruin, headlines, and other influences, became unknowingly embedded.

Architectural process and design inspiration can result from a very complex accumulation of seemingly unrelated experiences spanning one’s lifetime. These unconscious inspirations and long-forgotten experiences lie at the bottom of the mind like sediment connected only by the gathering weight of layers.

And then one day, a surface disturbance causes a disruption in the settlement, thereby causing a deviation in the main current. If I were a river this moment would be called an… eddy!

Lacey and I still work together, travel and debate. He still frustrates the shit out of me, but at my age, a disruption of sediment is... invigorating.

MASTERPLAN

Imagine having the financial resources to disband a Homeowner’s Association.

Almost every late twentieth century suburban development to the present has mandated the legalization of some form of governing authority usually referred to as the homeowner’s association. Eventually this name was reduced to an acronym: The “HOA.” Short and easy but no less annoying.

If a good architect is going to encounter resistance, ignorance and confrontation, it will be with the typically unqualified and irritatingly available members of the neighborhood HOA. This time it was the homeowner who said “enough.” When The Outpost was occupied there were four conventional houses existing within the eleven lot subdivision. After one too many letters from the HOA complaining about the unacceptable, unfinished nature of The Outpost architecture, Lacey bought five out of the six remaining lots. His bold covert action gave him a total of six out of eleven home sites and a permanent majority ownership. Wow!

Now there was an opportunity to look beyond a simple family residence and consider the planning possibilities of a larger neighborhood context. Although Lacey is no longer in the newspaper business he still remains the community activist and political agitator he has always been. Respecting compliance with local zoning requirements, the lots were studied as legally independent building sites each with a separate yet related program for an expanding art collection, “think tank” policy discussions, artist residence and a James Turrell Skyspace.

At this time, I did not know Mr. Turrell wanted to talk with me too!

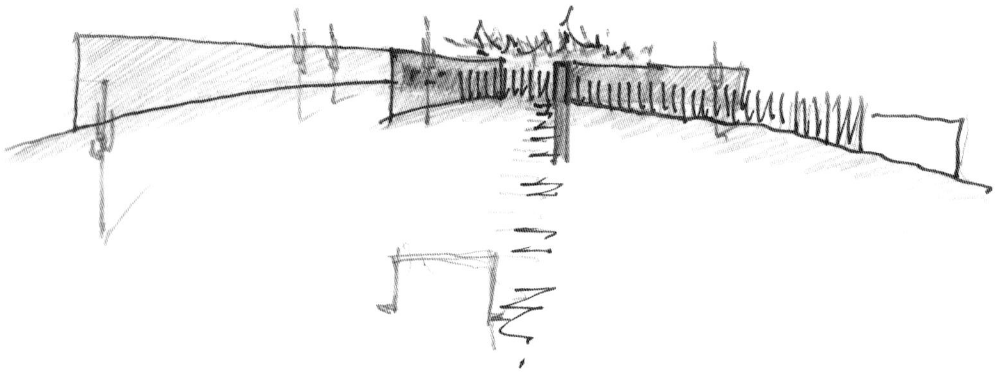

3300

165

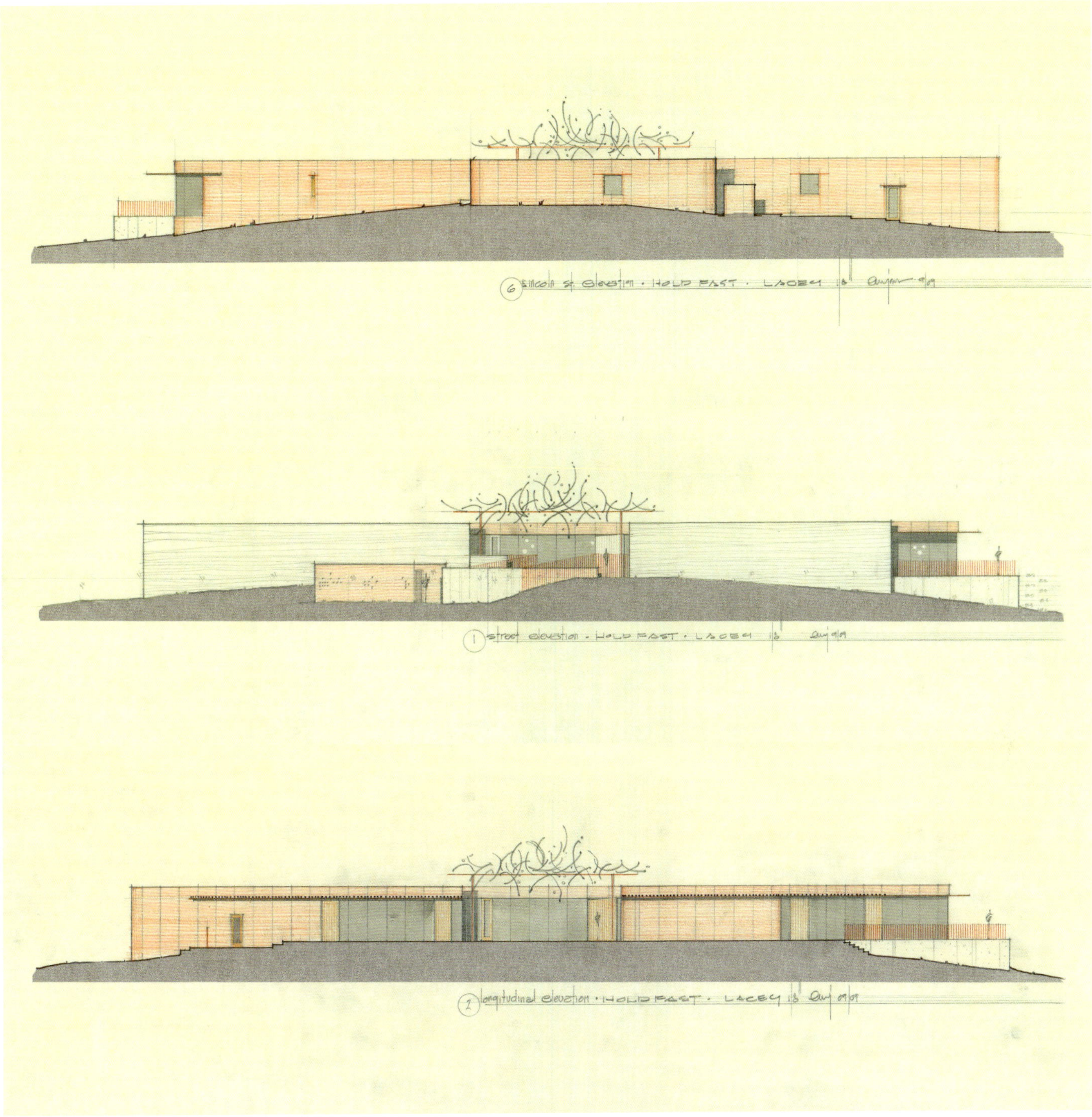
6 lincoln st elevation · HOLD FAST · LACEY
1 street elevation · HOLD FAST · LACEY
2 longitudinal elevation · HOLD FAST · LACEY

169

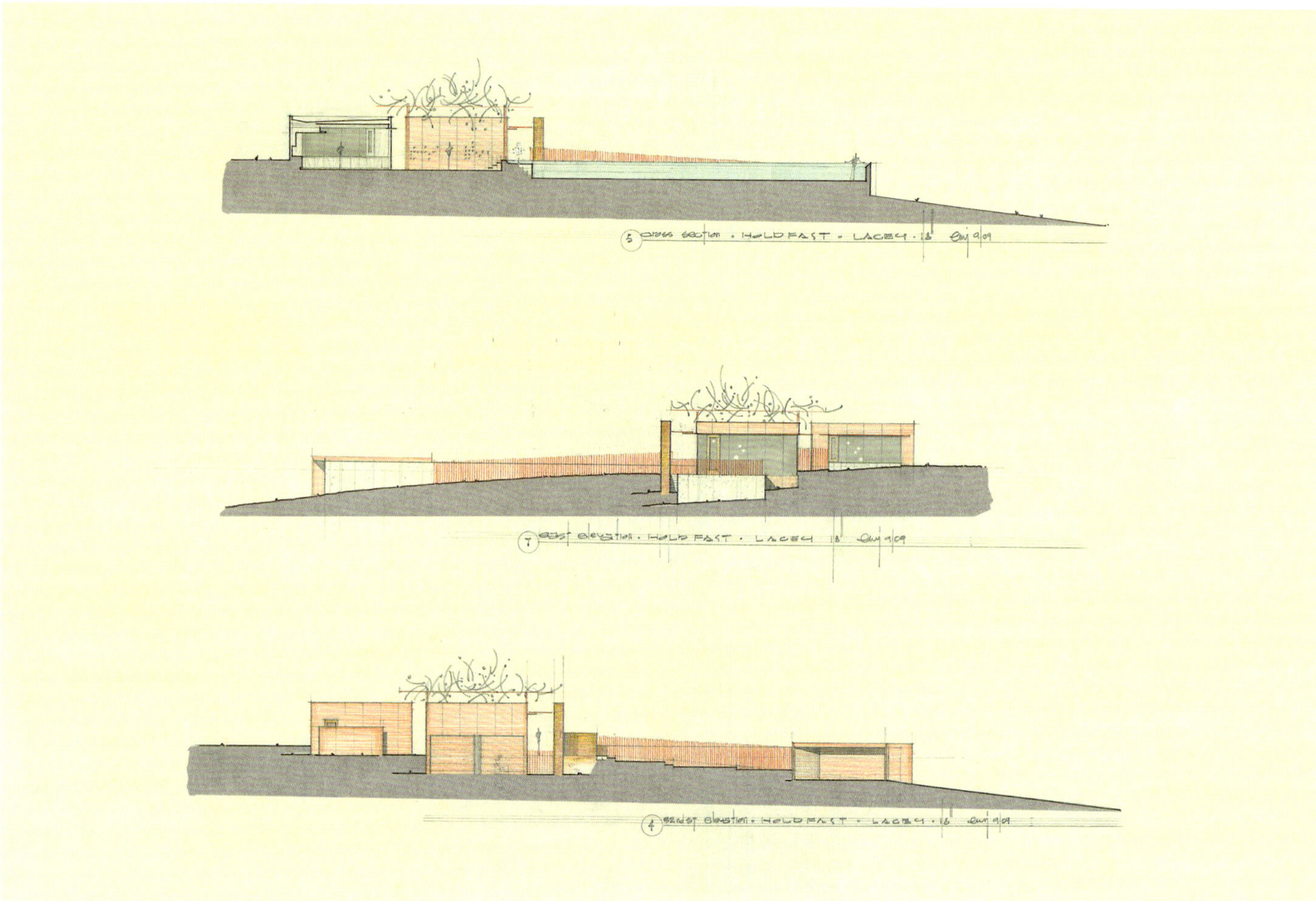
cross section · HOLDFAST · LACEY
east elevation · HOLDFAST · LACEY
west elevation · HOLDFAST · LACEY

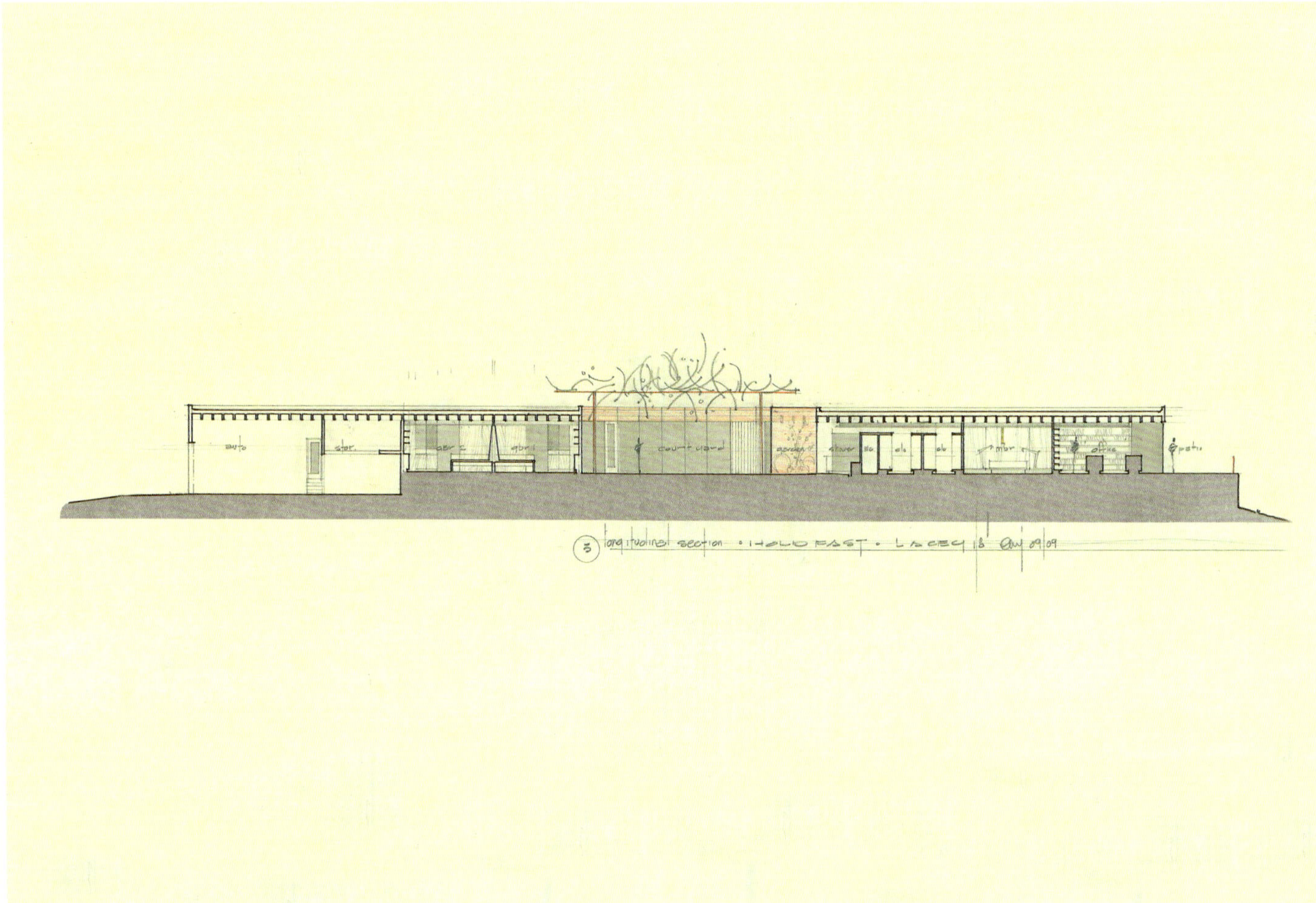
courtyard
garden
shower
mbr
3
longitudinal section

182

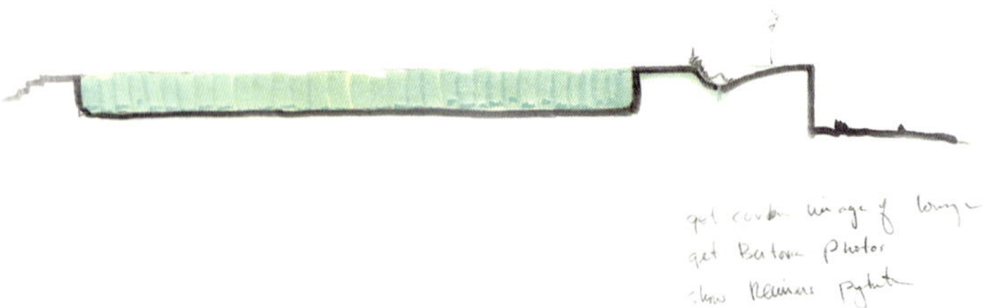

"Eddie Jones is a rare talent, an inspiring teacher and a committed citizen. He has integrated his broad array of talents, skills and interests to serve his community and profession through a body of work that is innovative, beautifully crafted, environmentally responsive and culturally resonant."

Buzz Yudell

FAIA (Moore Ruble Yudell). 2007 American Institute of Architects Los Angeles Gold Medal. 2006 National American Institute of Architects Firm of the Year.

Casa del Nido Osprey

Puerto Peñasco, México
/ 2009

Travel is our best education!

An exposure to foreign culture and the personal enrichment of experiencing ancient architecture can trigger a journey of discovery. Recognizing the qualities of weight, proportion, light, shadow, history, and material patina can feel like a revelation.

Casa del Nido Osprey is an expression of fundamentals… the exploration and subsequent interpretation of what an architect has learned. For example, the basic courtyard house is more about "finding" the secret garden than a program surrounding an outdoor space. It is about the lure of reflected light from an unseen source as it beckons one to enter. It is the untouchable sky made tangible by the context of a parapet's edge.

Then there is the arch. Common and overused in southwest suburban America, the arch has been reduced to a cliché. Once a milestone in structural innovation, it is now only understood as a semblance. However, when the arch is a space beyond an outline, the sunlight finds its dance partner, the brick finds its vault and the view thanks its gentle frame.

México! Simple contrasts, undulating dunes, level sea. Blue daytime horizon waits for another brilliantly colored sunset. Fuzzy saltbush against the straight edge parapet rhymes with the ragged steel rebar sculpture, honoring the local building traditions of the coastal osprey bird. The weightless sand blows easily against the heavy walls. Thick arches make a deep, protective shadow, defending against the searing white Mexican sunlight. The fascinating Sea of Cortez never stops moving, the beach is never the same. One is acutely aware of the consistency of change. The architecture tries desperately to remain static… and happily fails.

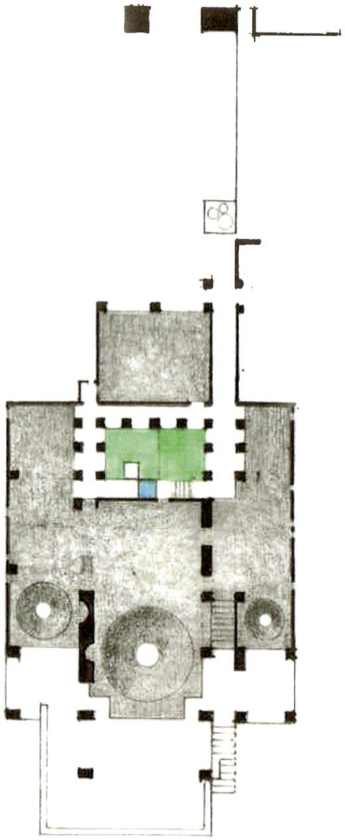

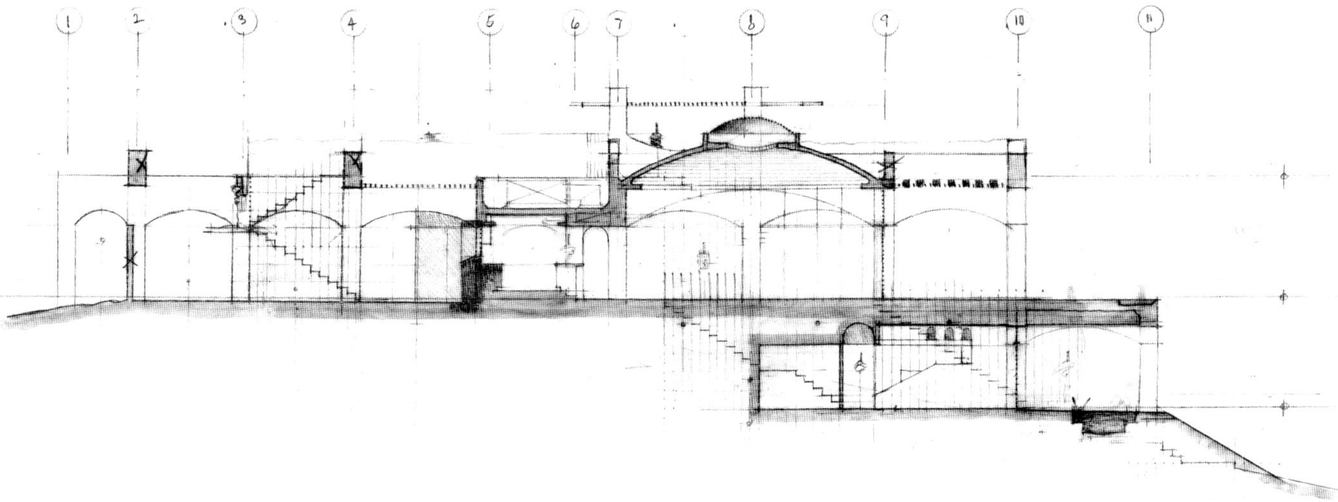
1
2
3
4
5
6
7
8
9
10
11

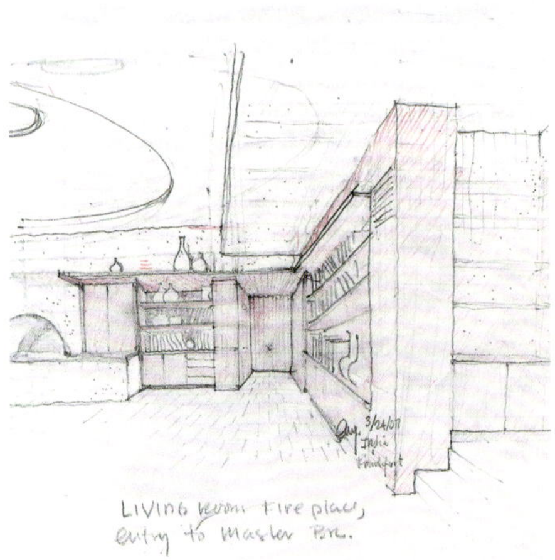
3/24/07
LIVING Room Fire place,
entry to Master Br.

“Eddie Jones is an architectural Shaman, capturing the magic of the Arizona desert with light and shadow. His work inspires contemplation, summons emotion, and connects people to nature, each other, and themselves.”

Steven Ehrlich

FAIA, Founding Partner (Ehrlich Yanai Rhee Chaney Architects). 2015 National American Institute of Architects Firm of the Year.

Logan Collection

Scottsdale, Arizona
/ 2008

"I want a place for my art collection – then I want to live there."
Kent Logan

The Logan House is first a private museum, second, a personal winter residence. Their art is among the top one hundred contemporary collections in the United States, and the architect vowed the architecture would be an equally significant addition.

After several studies, it was mutually decided the program would be about multiple galleries, each with a different daylighting technique.

Passage below the metallic "golden aspen leaves" provides transitional entry shade and recalls landscape surrounding the couple's Vail, Colorado summer residence. Upon passing through the front door, guests enter Gallery One. The Sonoran Desert is well known for its clear light; however, it must be diffused to avoid damaging the art. Six foot deep, parabolic white plaster shafts bounce and reflect light, evenly distributing it throughout the space. Skylights begin as circular oculi, warp to a square, and integrate an adjustable electric lighting grid, which doubles as the mounting point for suspended walls of art, subject to relocation as needed.

Gallery Two is easily perceived from the exterior as a glowing cube. Natural light is diffused through laminated glass film, then a six foot cavity reflecting light up and down, and finally filtered through a white, stretched fabric ceiling. Gallery Three – the "black box" – has only a hint of natural light, penetrating through the iris of a sandblasted eye pattern integrated into the exterior cast-in-place concrete walls. Architecturally, the eyes are used to strategically identify spaces in the house that contain only art. Gallery Four's exaggerated linear shape accommodates the famous thirty-foot-long Takashi Murakami painting; *Supernova* is naturally lit from a parallel clerestory above which gathers north light to reflect off the opposite white bulkhead.

The fractured yet orthogonal building footprint assures the very least site disruption. Every Saguaro cactus was saved. Every boulder, Palo Verde tree, and contour was preserved. This claim is only possible when the architecture is inspired by its subordination to the landscape!

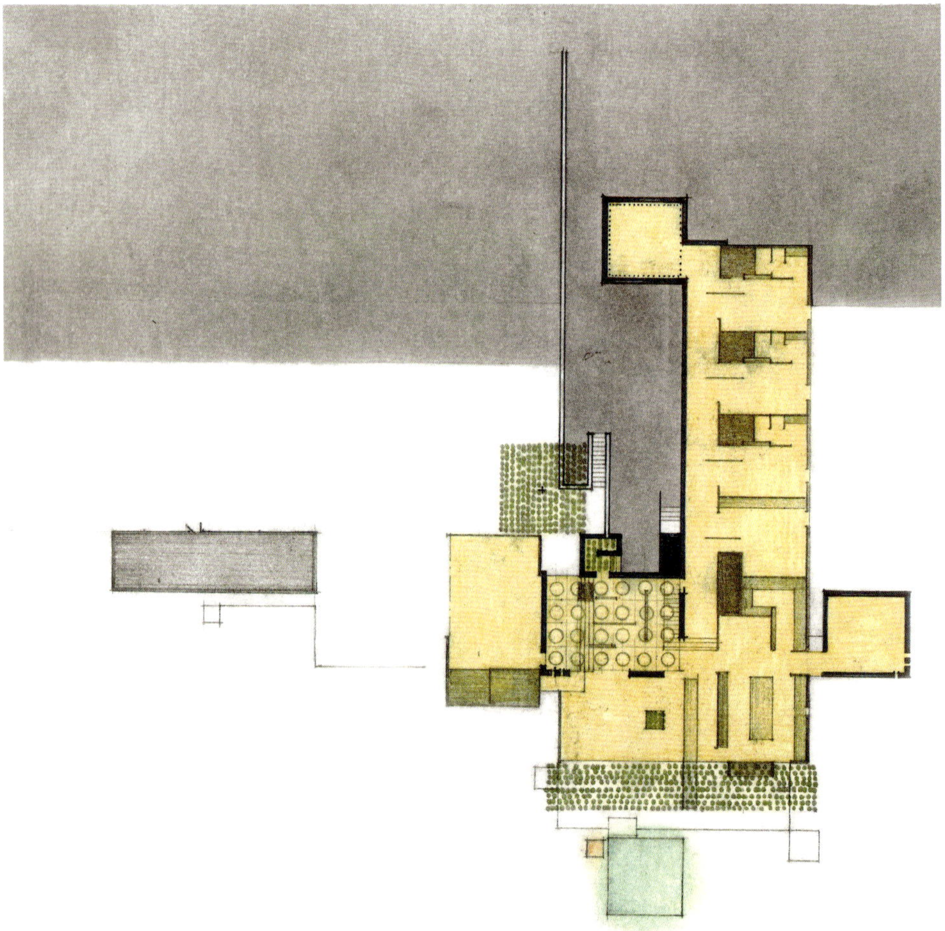

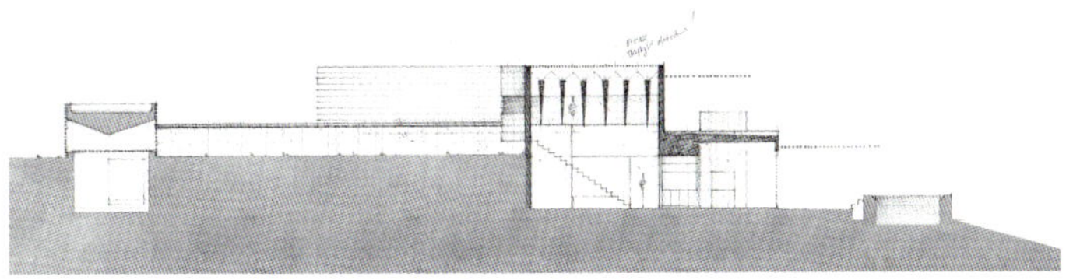

HI-STANDARD

Hennessy

"In Eddie's hands the sustainable becomes a phenomenally based architectural experience of the highest order. Using color, and varied translucencies, his projects animate the harsh southern sun with sometimes playful, sometimes serene effect."

Julie V. Snow

FAIA (Snow Kreilich Architects). 2018 National American Institute of Architects Firm of the Year.

Scorpion

Scottsdale, Arizona
/ 2002

Hillside contours, boulder field, distant views, and stands of old Saguaro shape the cast-in-place concrete ledge. Interlocking with the curvilinear retaining walls, a protective shell of oxidized titanium plates integrates the "scorpion" form with desert shadow.

An inverted conical-shaped roof unifies the continuous interior, defends against a western solar exposure and responds to the incline of the land. Multiple center points are subordinate to the radial joint grid generated by the hemispherical pool. Program elements are directed to, across, and beyond the seemingly suspended disc of blue water leaking through a coping sleeve of two hundred fifty-four stainless steel nipples.

Although the entry sequence straddles a small, yet significant canyon, the resulting upper landing bridge allows the existing drainage pattern to continue undisturbed. The beautiful arroyo view is only revealed after ascending the stair and passing through the creature's concrete backbone.

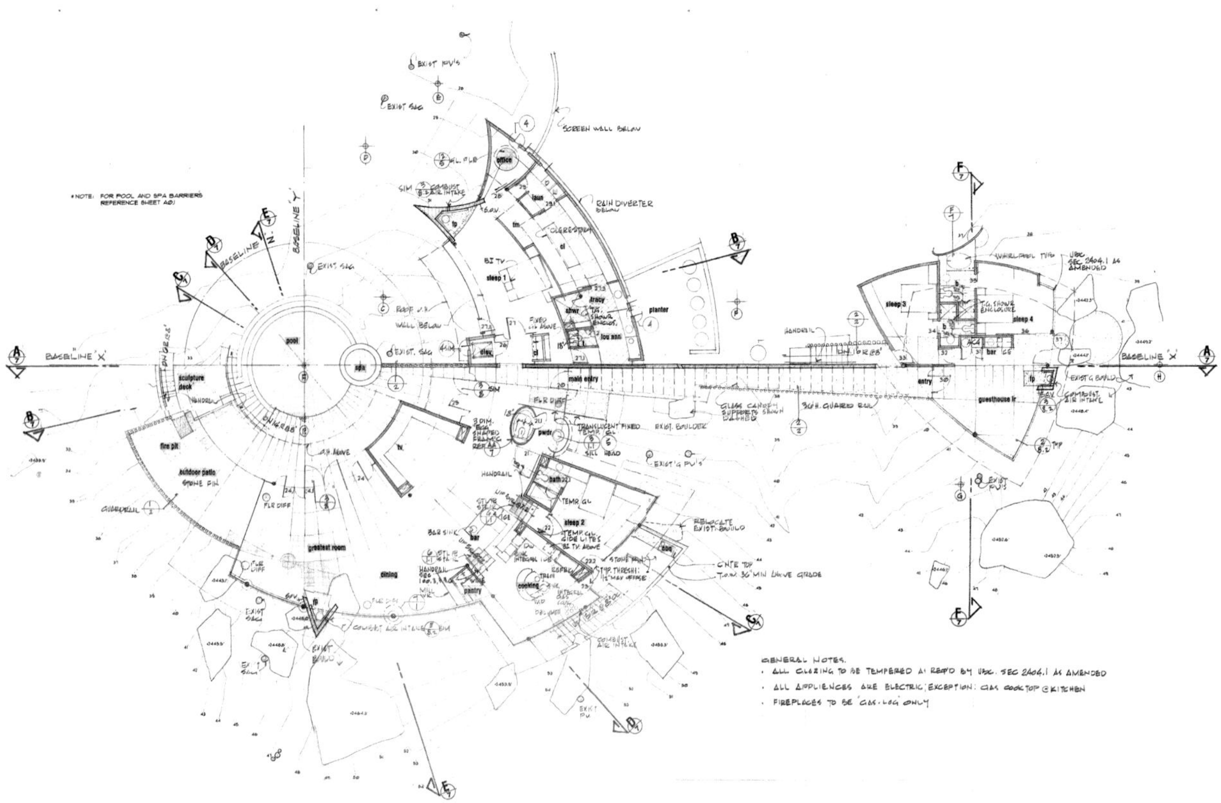

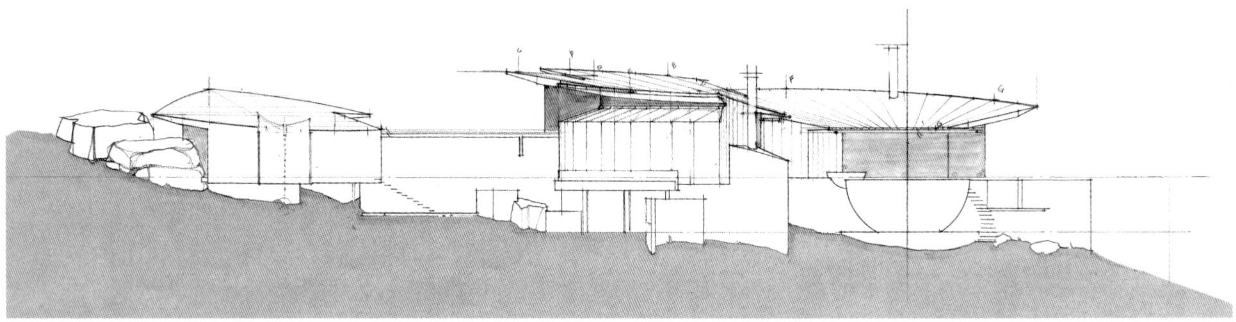

Drawing by Julian Clark

“ON MY MIND - today and tomorrow.

Eddie Jones is a rebel.

Standing middle distance, focusing on what was in front of me, the Architecture became more exuberant, more enriched, in detail and form.

The simplicity from the back distance was still present, but unexpectedly, it was simplicity on the other side of complexity.

There was more to see, not in addition to, but as an unfolding of larger elements of form first seen from a greater distance away.

Moving closer yet, the foreground yielded another reality of texture, coloration and seams, given a deeper meaning with the binary of solid-void and visual gradients of transparency.

My eyes never wandering, never turning my head, was the only way to satisfy an inquiring mind, ‘was it possible to see more and more, moving forward at a steady slow pace, focusing on one point, as the architecture unfolded before my eyes.’

Only possible, I thought, if the Architect had the same degree of focus and concentration coupled with a highly skilled hand and the architectural knowledge intuited moment to moment throughout the creative process.

The architecture stands its ground, but in a quiet way.

It is soft spoken but self-assured, confident.

It speaks in silence, like the master and guest in a tea ceremony.

Yes, this is certainly simplicity on the other side of complexity.

Distilled, waiting for the arrival of someone with no preconceptions and great patience, whose palette is every sense integrated into one sense, like Thoreau on a particular fall evening.

Freeman Dyson, the physicist, once conveyed to his colleagues, that you cannot be a self-respecting scientist without being a rebel.

The same holds true for Architects.

Eddie Jones is a rebel."

Michael Rotondi

(Roto Architects). Co-Founder of The Southern California Institute of Architecture (SCI-ARC), 1972. Co-Founder of Morphosis Architects, 1976-1991.

House of Five Dreams

Paradise Valley, Arizona
/ 2001

A pair of prolific art collectors desired to consolidate their art and artifacts from two locations across the country to one new place. As their passion evolved from merely a hobby to a full-time profession, the couple decided to have their residence physically separated from the exhibition experience, yet co-located, thereby organizing their lives in a new way. Although the collection is private, scholars and aficionados visit often, and pieces come and go on loan on a regular basis. A new gallery would need to efficiently and beautifully store and display each piece, with complete flexibility for growth and change.

The project has three distinct parts, each with its own material palette and function.

Because the majority of the artifacts have been, at one time or another, excavated from the ground, the decision was made to place the gallery spaces below grade. This would help maintain a constant temperature and lower energy costs. In addition, sinking twenty thousand square feet would greatly diminish the perceived size of the dwelling, putting it in scale with the surrounding neighborhood houses. Given that a large hole would be dug to create the space, it made sense to surround the gallery with rammed-earth retaining walls using the material excavated on site. Every material below the horizon, would be completely "natural"—raw rammed earth, raw steel, raw concrete, raw wood, etc.

We floated their new residence above the ground as high as allowed by zoning. The materials in this elevated single story are "synthetic"—glass, terrazzo, stainless steel, and other types of reflective material. The reflections would bring light and views of the surrounding sky, mountains and city deep into the house, creating a sensation of hovering in space.

In between the two main levels, one enters where one inhabits the horizon. Views are carefully manipulated to only see inward. The materials from both levels meld and create a surreal point of contact with framed mountain views and the owners' full art collection. Additionally, this three-sto-

ry vertical circulation element is dominated by a 72 foot long, 25 foot tall handmade, undulating, stacked glass wall. The many thousands of horizontal glass layers reinforce the idea of the horizon, while reflecting and refracting light like... a jewel!

One descends below the ground surface. The horizon line seems to rise. You move deeper. Light levels reduce, sound reverberation increases, temperature drops. There is an awareness of the damp smell of soil. You are in the room; a large room sharing an amazing collection of artifacts discovered underground, buried thousands of years before, now visible, yet still below the ground. The natural insulating qualities of the earth keep the room comfortable. The mass of the earth can be felt. Time to go home. Ascension. Up into a cloud space, diffuse bright light everywhere, high above the ground where all things are possible!

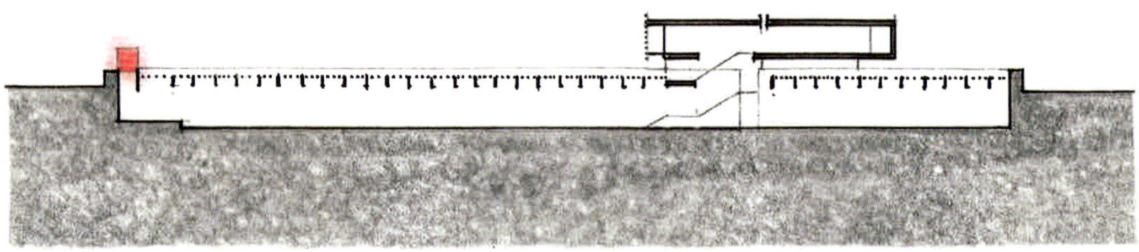

274

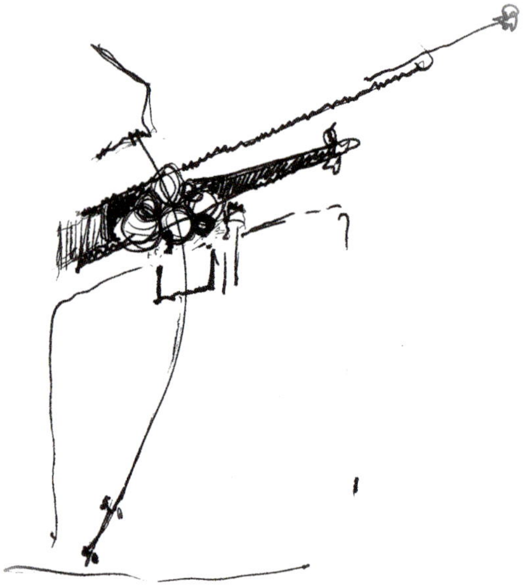

282

“Like us, Eddie was addressing sustainability before it was seen as a global imperative.

“Our firm and others were inspired by what we saw happening in the desert.”

Julie Eizenberg

FAIA, Principal (KoningEizenberg). 2019 Australian Institute of Architects Gold Medal. AIA California Council Firm of the Year Award.

“Guy de Maupassant pointed out, back in 1884, ‘The human mind is capable of anything.’ Here is evidence: the mind – and spirit – of architect Eddie Jones makes extraordinary environments of light and space, surrounded by materials everyone knows about but only Jones puts together in this way. Capable of anything! And they all really work. What a delight.”

Jeff Stein

President of the Cosanti Foundation. Former Co-President of Arcosanti.

Johnson Jones

Phoenix, Arizona
/ 2000

How does an architect tolerate living in suburbia? As with any community, there are opportunities growing in the cracks of conformity waiting to be recognized.

Ahwatukee, Crow word for "House of Dreams," is a suburban Phoenix, Arizona neighborhood attempting to dominate the southern base of a magnificent mountain preserve known locally as South Mountain Park. The idea for protecting this area dates back to 1924, and to this day, South Mountain Park remains the largest municipal park in the United States.

In 1929 Frank Lloyd Wright completed plans for the San Marcos-in-the-Desert Resort. It was never built. The site was located at the southern base of South Mountain, and in 1997 the only private property left from the original resort location had been scraped to build the naked berm desperately pretending to conceal the forty-foot diameter neighborhood water chlorination tank. No one knew this was a historical site and no one wanted a residential lot looking at a giant steel cylinder.

Perfect. The price was right!

The architectural question was not how to fit into the existing built context. The aspiration was to honor the 17,000-acre backyard and repair the site. Clearly, the question was how to continue a progressive lifestyle in an architecture surrounded by conventional houses.

In suburbia, everything is new... even when it's not! The inspiration for rammed earth construction could easily be assumed to be grounded in the lessons of Arizona's indigenous people. After all, Casa Grande Ruins National Monument is over 750 years old.[1] When one builds new among the perpetual new, one may choose to disassociate with the bewilderment of mindless beige and pink tile roofs. Hence, the dirt walls. Although new, they were instantly old by embedding the results of a million years of geographical history throughout its monolithic construct. We completely restored

the site and the architecture harvests infrequent desert rainfall. We delighted in our environmentally responsible example and moved in April 1999.

To this day, I can discern no apparent influence on subsequent Ahwatukee residential infill. But, it's okay. We crunch along our entry walk, pass through a weathered wooden gate into a beautiful cylindrical composed courtyard, a shape not unlike the water tank. Then we disappear into our private world of critters, rock formations and desert light, which, philosophically, parallels the entry experience of an old Mexican hacienda. Convention is out of sight... out of mind.

On this land, there was once a promise of desert architecture uniquely reflecting Sonoran magic, still present in 1999. The Johnson-Jones house proudly stakes out its small territory and serves as a steward preserving one small piece of the promise.

1 A little less than halfway between Phoenix and Tucson, Casa Grande Ruins National Monument preserves the remains of one of the largest prehistoric structures ever constructed in North America, built by the ancestral Sonoran Desert people.

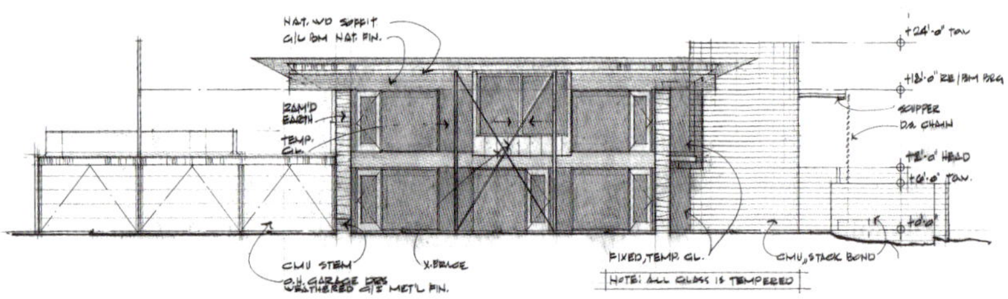

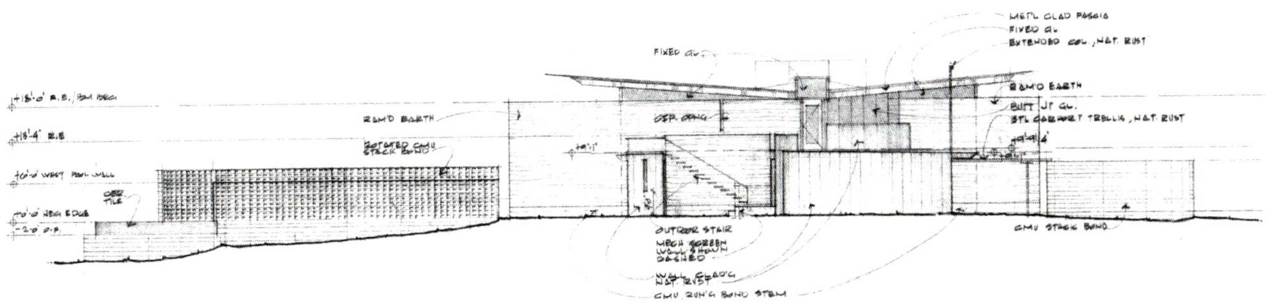
METL CLAD FASCIA
FIXED GL.
EXTENDED COL, NAT. RUST
RAM'D EARTH
BUTT JT GL.
RAM'D EARTH
OUTDOOR STAIR
CMU STACK BOND

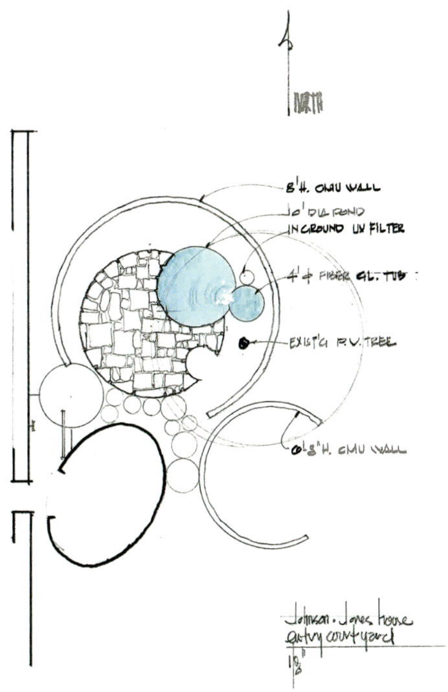
NORTH
8'H. CMU WALL
10' DIA POND
INGROUND UV FILTER
EXIST'G P.V. TREE
Johnson . Jones house
entry courtyard

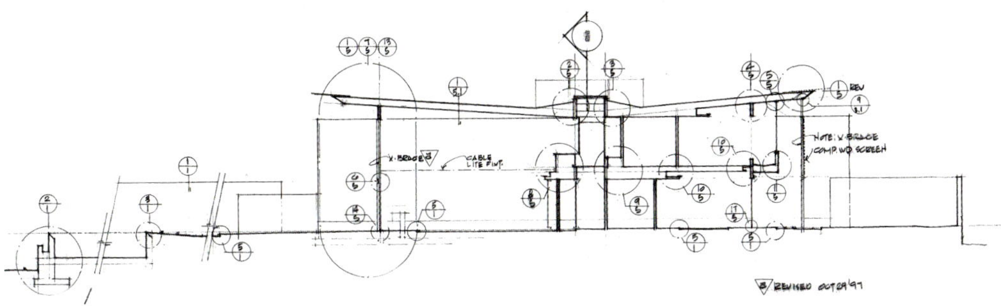

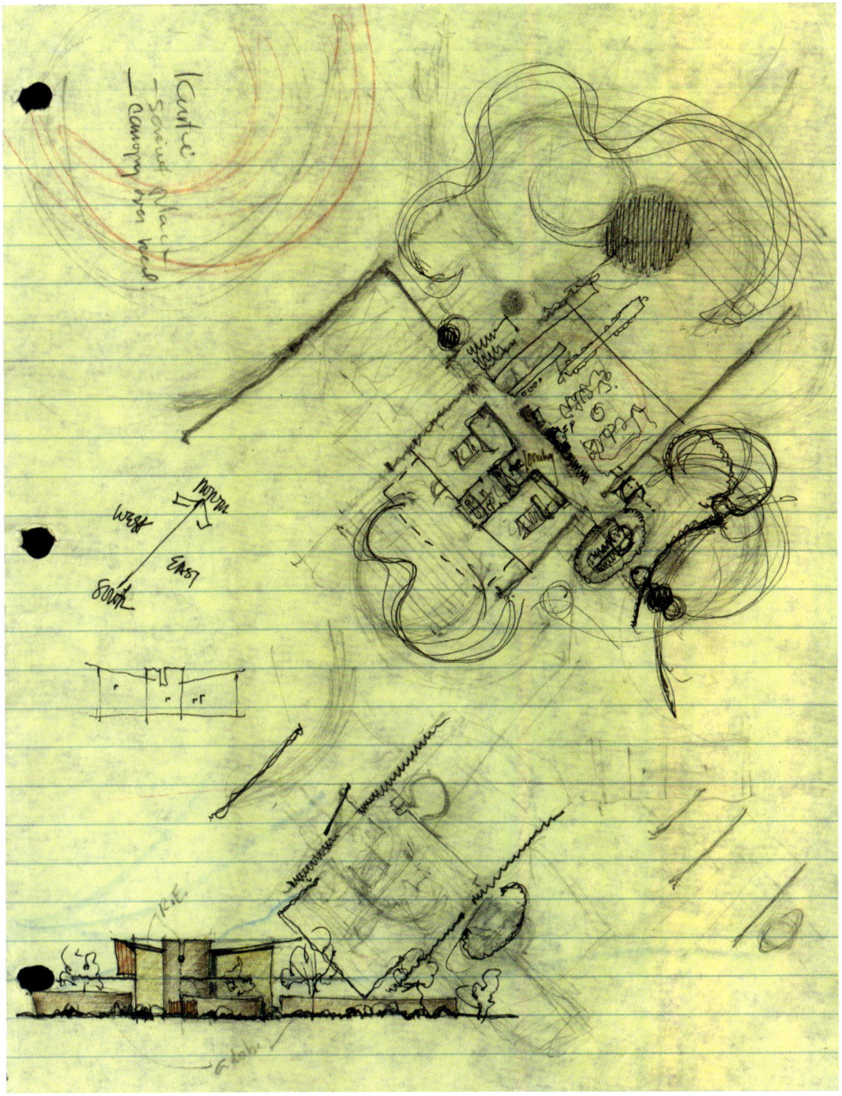
NORTH
WEST
EAST
SOUTH

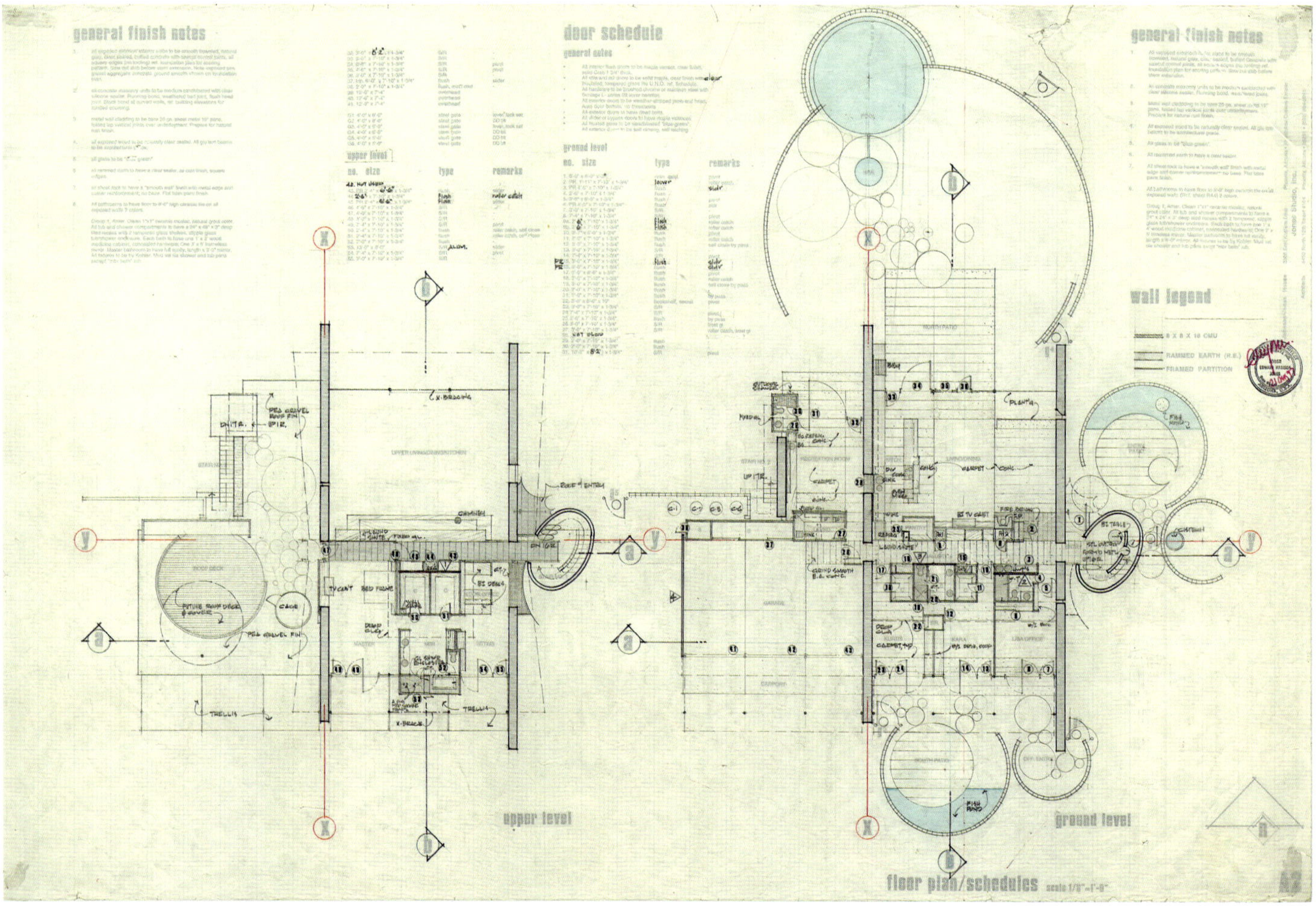
general finish notes
door schedule
general finish notes
wall legend
upper level
ground level
floor plan/schedules

In Conversation

Eddie Jones with Vladimir Belogolovsky

“What Is Architecture for if Not to Embrace and Excite Its Community?”

In conversation with Eddie Jones By Vladimir Belogolovksy

September 4, 2020

Vladimir Belogolovsky Your buildings have something I have never seen before – eyelashes. I am referring to metal overhangs bent into a sort of fingers framing the windows. Some houses have these eyelashes in metal, steel, and others in wood. Could you talk about them and how did you come up with this eccentric idea?

Eddie Jones When Frank Lloyd Wright first arrived in Arizona, he intuitively knew the desert was about dotted lines, as opposed to straight edges. If you look at Taliesin West there is a fascia dentil, as seen in ancient Greek and Roman temples. In most of his Arizona houses you will see a similar dentil making a dotted line. And what you refer to as eyelashes, has to do with that idea. My intention was to cast intriguing shadows. I said, “How can I make a fuzzy line?” It was easy! We used a water jet cutter to slice the metal overhang edge of the Charles Drive House (figure on the opposite page) then bent the fingers up and down. It was only when we finished, was I reminded of eyelashes. In another example, the Starwood Residence in Montana (page 132), we cut the stainless steel roof edge to catch snow and form a necklace of icicles that would glisten in sunlight. It's a beautiful thing. The Outpost (page 174) uses randomly cantilevered wood boards to dissipate the edges into air. I projected the Scorpion House (page 264) roof gutter to clear rain runoff away from the elevated deck. Result? The roof edge embraces the sky. Here I must bring up the name of my other hero – Bruce Goff who probably influenced my work as much as Wright. He never gave up. He was enthusiastic about starting over. If something was too expensive or he missed a certain mark, he would develop a different idea and then, another one. You never knew what he was going to do next. And I hope you will never know what I am going to do next. I don't claim that's the way to do architecture. But it's my way. And it is fun; I am never bored.

VB I read that when you were just a boy you were interested in floor plans. I think the only way you could come across such things as floor plans if you grew up in the family of an architect. Did you?

EJ No, I didn't. My mother subscribed to women's magazines such as *Ladies' Home Journal, House Beautiful, and Good Housekeeping.* And believe it or not, in the 50's they would publish plans of modern houses every month. These houses were very different from the one I lived in. Almost always, they would have a low pitched roof and floor to ceiling glass. You could see out. You could breathe. I imagined I would feel uplifted and free. Even as a child, I was naturally drawn to them, and I would try to guess – where in the floor plan were the photos taken. It was my game. When my father bought the 26 volume set of Encyclopedia Britannica, I looked at every single page in every book from A to Z. When I got to the W's there was Wright and his masterpiece, Fallingwater. That did it. It communicated to me directly, particularly on an emotional level. I was only six years old!

VB You were born in Texas, raised in Oklahoma, and studied architecture at Oklahoma State University. How was your experience at the university?

EJ I had a wonderful experience at that school. Girls finally started noticing me! But remember, this was the late 1960s and we were protesting everything. There was one professor, Wayne Bartels who was very avant-garde. He worked with me to open my eyes. I was really searching for answers, "What is this thing called architecture?" What do they mean when they say, "The light is everything?" Because of this persistent questioning I can honestly say I am mostly self-taught. Not that I don't have influences. I read, I engage in discussions, I travel, and I continue searching. Traveling is particularly important. For example, I went to Havana, Cuba three times. Interestingly, most people see the city's deterioration in a negative way. And it is a shame this beautiful city is crumbling. But for me it was a realization that there is an entire city the Earth is reclaiming. It is nature that has been the designer there for the last half century. There is something poetic and honest about accepting the inevitable. Yet, so many people are preoccupied with throwing money at expensive maintenance to deny the fact their structures are getting old. My favorite buildings are the ones that are aging gracefully. Who does not like an Italian hill town? You don't paint it; you just let it be. I also enjoyed a trip to India. I explored temples and stepwells. There is something powerful about ancient architecture that communicates with everyone on a very basic level. The architecture seems to grow out of the rock. Architecture and nature become one and seamless.

All of this makes me think about my own work. Of course, I appreciate Modernism and the desire to make buildings as light and as transparent as possible. My generation was particularly influenced by the Case Study House program in Los Angeles. But I am also influenced by the opposite, where the ratio between mass and void is completely reversed. I find something very meaningful, fundamental, and humanistic about it. So, these trips made me rethink my own work and starting from about 30 years ago, it became heavier and protected. In a way, I matured and progressed beyond pure Modernism. I was bored with pointy metal buildings. It was then I began to respect vernacular, historical precedents, materials and construction techniques. If you had my education and travel experience you can't possibly be a conservative because your eyes open, your mind expands, and you want to try so many things in new ways. I actually have a ferocious appetite for experiencing new architecture. I am 71, but I will knock on a complete stranger's door if I see something of interest! I will sneak onto private property just to inhale a unique work of architecture, even if I can only be there for a moment. I have done that all over the world. Because I am naïve, I am morally immune to the possible consequences of trespassing laws.

VB How did you discover Arizona and why did you decide to live your life there?

EJ I was seduced by the images of magical Arizona sunsets in *Arizona Highways* magazine, which was the best tool to attract tourists that any state ever produced. Also, Taliesin West was here and Paolo Soleri's Arcosanti. To be honest, I didn't need much of an excuse because I wanted to get out of Oklahoma. I had to find something new. I was suffocating as a young graduate. So, in 1973, I drove my pathetic Volkswagen Beetle 1,000 miles to the Sonoran Desert in Phoenix in August. Man, was it hot! It's as simple as that. I am glad I did it and living here this long, I have witnessed an incredible transformation of a major city. I have participated in this process. I know the mayor and local community leaders. I have to be involved. Coming here was not about courage. It wasn't about frustration. It was about naiveté. We already had a two-year-old son, Christopher. I was crazy to move away from all the grandparents in Oklahoma City. But I was determined. I had to leave. I never looked back.

First, I worked for the oldest architectural firm in Arizona. I learned a lot in the five years I was there. But I did not enjoy it. I was a good designer. But my designs would be taken away and developed by others in the office, and they would be diluted. By the time my designs were taken to the field to be built, they were murdered. [Laughs.] They were dead buildings. People at the office would tell me, "There are so many codes; you can't fight it." I didn't believe that for a second. I compensated by making up hypothetical projects (page 14) to design on my own time. I have always been good at drawing. It gives me joy. Even to this day, architecture has never been real work for me. I am lucky. I believe it is not anyone's responsibility to make others happy. I have to take responsibility. So, when my then wife, Mary, lost her job after I bought a Jensen-Healey sports car, I quit the firm. I couldn't take it anymore. Of course, I had to sell the car. And guess what? The guy who bought the car asked me, "What do you do for living?" Once I told him I was an architect (I exaggerated! I was in the process of getting licensed) he said, "Well, I want to build a new house. Would you like to design it?" I said, "Sure!" [Laughs.] I had never done a building on my own before. I was so naïve. I did it anyway. We came over budget. So, the client said, "Why don't we build it ourselves?! You know how to do it, right?" Again, I said, "Sure!" [Laughs.] Of course, I had never been a general contractor before. That experience became an extension of my education at Oklahoma State University. This first job became extremely important to me because I had to do everything myself with my own hands. I had to hire people, fire them. It took a year and a half to finish the job. It was tough but fulfilling work. The house was called the Tatham Residence; it was built on the side of a hill with dry-stacked block retaining walls in 1979. It is still there.

VB You just said that you like to make up projects, working on them on your own time and you continue doing that. Do you mean that even now you keep working on idea projects that may not be realized?

EJ Of course! I have a wonderful story about that. I once was master planning a neighborhood with an intention to commission a James Turrell Skyspace as the focal point (page 163). You wouldn't believe it – one day Turrell called me! It was for a completely different reason. I had no idea he knew about me. He is like a God. In my opinion, he is probably the most important artist in the world. And his Roden Crater is in Arizona. So, when he phoned and said he wanted to talk to me, I responded, "And there is something I want to discuss with you!" So, he said, "Can you come up tomorrow?" I dropped everything and drove to Flagstaff, which is 150 miles north of Phoenix. We had lunch and then we drove to Roden Crater. Wow! We spent eight hours together, continuing to dusk. He said, "Don't look at the sunset; look at the night rising." He taught me how to see night rising! Anyway, the reason he wanted to see me, as he explained, was his idea to choose six architects to design six houses for individuals who would agree to live there for two months of the year, while the rest of the time, these houses would act as artist's residences. He asked me not to reveal the five other architects, but you know them. And a short while later, while in Southern Italy for a one-month-long summer vacation at a 700-year-old villa, I jumped at the opportunity to design this dream project without waiting for the reality of a commission. We would travel daily along the Amalfi Coast – Sorrento, Positano, Ravello; we went to Capri every week. It was a very stimulating trip. Still, I couldn't simply be there for a long time without working on a project. And that's what I did. I chose to design the residence that James had dangled in my face. I loved every minute working on it. When I came back, I called James and said, "I know you didn't ask me to move ahead and develop a design, but consider it my gift to you for spending so much time with me. You can use it or not, anyway you like." He invited me for dinner in Winslow! That was good enough. It was about five years ago, and I am still the only architect out of the selected shortlist who attempted a design. I get to say, "James Turrell has my drawings in his collection!" (page 339).

VB I hope there is still a future for that project. Wouldn't it be the point and worth your effort?

EJ Hell yes! But the point of this story is my idea is out there. If I waited for a real client, that project might never be imagined. In my early days, I would go home and make stuff up to preserve my sanity. I can still do that, although my motivations are different. I can use these thought exercises for my lectures, potential projects, or teaching assignments. Once I asked University of Oklahoma students to design an artist residence at Roden Crater without knowing who is coming – a writer, painter, sculptor. How do you make it particular to the family that will live there and subsequent guest artists? Plus, you have a responsibility to relate the house to the Crater, a breathtaking example of Earth art. There are so many unique challenges you may never encounter in your life. That's why it is important to test oneself against extraordinary constraints. That's what I like most – to respond to unique challenges. You must pose unique questions and the answers will follow. So, I see these made-up projects of mine as very useful. But in the past, I would simply do them for pure pleasure.

VB Could you talk about your design studio near the Arizona State University campus? In a way, it operates as a sort of culture hub and community center, right?

EJ Absolutely. It would be selfish not to use our new Studio in that way! (page 28) The land was very affordable because it is located in the flight path of Phoenix Sky Harbor International Airport. Yet, it is within walking distance of the Arizona State University campus, light rail, and restaurants. Although it is in an underserved neighborhood in Tempe, it is starting to change, thanks in part to our investment. What is architecture for if not to embrace and excite its community? There are 15 of us working here. I have been very fortunate to have had my younger brother Neal Jones as my partner since 1986. Neal's business acumen assured us a 40 year career. Around 6 years ago, Brian Farling and Jacob Benyi became partners and immediately started impacting the Studio's upward trajectory. The balance of the team is made up of the most wonderful men and women. Their talents are diverse, but we continue to be a tight knit family sharing common ethical standards and soaring aspiration.

One of the advantages of owning a building is I decide how to use it. When we work here, we give many tours to students and others. We host board meetings, community group gatherings, a lecture series, children's workshops and more. We don't charge and we don't say no to anyone. It is like a culture salon where people come to discuss interesting topics. In collaboration with "Spirit of the Senses", a local intellectually engaged organization, we have hosted US Senators, Nobel Prize physicists, authors, artists, musicians, journalists and I am grateful to participate in these cultural exchanges. This place helps our community to express itself. Also, we like working in the public eye and exchanging ideas. For example, in 2006, we were asked to do a show at the Scottsdale Museum of Contemporary Art. Instead of investing our efforts in putting projects on a wall we moved our entire office into the gallery for a four month long exhibition! We pinned up our most representative projects for people to see, but more importantly it was about direct communication. All our consultants and clients came to the museum for meetings. It was a very engaging and fulfilling experience. A lot of parents brought their children and we talked to their kids about the joy of architecture. Many people had almost no knowledge of what architecture was, and hopefully, we had an impact on their interest through meaningful, direct conversations.

VB Let's talk about your design process and some of your inspirations.

EJ I don't allow myself to think about design until I am on-site. When I am there, paying attention to the forces, ideas will appear in my head. Associations and inspiration start swirling around. Sure, my client will give me all the requirements and the numbers. But it is the site that will tell me what the appropriate form and material palette will be. It works like this – client, site, solution. When you combine two ingredients – people and topography – you get architecture. This may sound overly simplistic, but it is based on intuition plus analysis, and my ability to relinquish my pencil to Mother Nature. I don't know why everybody doesn't think this way because it is so obvious. [Laughs.]

Speaking of inspiration, I would have to name not just architects as references, but also artists. For example, Vermeer paintings influence me in the amazing way he painted light, particularly how it dissipates on a wall surface. Or how Turrell introduces color without paint. His colors diffuse and gradually, materially evaporate. That's what guides me. I am smart enough to design space deliberately, knowing what the results will be. But, more often than not, I surprise myself. That's what is great about architecture; it allows nature or light to take over. Architecture is a combination of unexpected surprise and deliberateness.

VB I want you to talk more about your fascination with materials and how this may relate to expressing personal, original, and subjective ideas. And here I want to bring the importance of the work of Bruce Goff again, as well as his followers into our conversation. How did you discover his architecture and what are your feelings about his unique buildings?

EJ I first encountered his work as a child. It was customary for my family to go on Sunday drives to see various neighborhoods. And one day my dad said, "You know, there is a really screwy house under construction. Let's go see it!" It was a bizarre thing in a very conventional neighborhood. And once I saw it, I would always ask my parents, "Let's go see the screwy house!" So, I watched it being built. And when I was in college, I saw Goff's Pollock House in our library. Later, my dad told me about another strange house in Norman, a suburb south of Oklahoma City where we lived. A fantastic house where everything was suspended off a recycled oil field drill stem; a central mast, 55 feet high. The house had a single spiraling wall and no interior partitions, just a series of platforms at different heights. That was, of course, the Bavinger House. My God, there has never been anything like the Bavinger House before or since. It was completely unique, original architecture. Very tragically, it no longer exists but I got to experience it. So, ever since college, I wanted to meet Goff. It was actually not that hard – two years before his death, I dialed his number, my brother Neal and I drove to Tyler, Texas and we spent a whole day talking at his home.

And very close to Goff's Bavinger House was another house in Norman by Goff's student Herb Greene nicknamed the "Prairie Chicken" (page 52). It was Greene's first house. When I first saw it, I was shocked and thrilled. This building; this haystack of weathered wood; this pile of ragged 1x lumber felt like wooden poetry! And the poem owned me, triggering distant thoughts, creating confusion, then revelation. Finally, it began to haunt me. It is still an influence. Herb no longer lived there but I tried to get inside for more than 40 years. Every time I went to Oklahoma for Christmas, I would travel to Norman, knock on the door, but the mean old woman would not let me in. Then she died two years ago. Guess who took me into the house? Herb Greene himself! We met at his University of Oklahoma lecture and we've been friends ever since. He doesn't practice architecture anymore. He is a wonderful artist and architect, and the day he showed me his "Prairie House," I actually cried! That house is the closest thing to an Oklahoma vernacular architecture you can get. Yet, it doesn't look like anything anybody has ever seen. It has been a very influential house in my life. And my "Prairie Raptor" house (page 90) in Oklahoma City is a direct result of the "Prairie House."

VB Could you get into some specifics about the influences of Goff on your work?

EJ The materials. When I was younger, I thought I couldn't do anything with the right angle. I thought boxes were sacrilegious and I must explore unusual geometry. And I did. I designed quite a few, one could say "Goffian" projects. But, I matured and my work became more disciplined. Yet, my fascination with materials used in unusual, novel ways has remained. What Goff taught me was everything is beautiful within the right context. He had such a wild, child-like imagination – using anything from large blue pieces of glass cullet to packing peanuts and razor blades. He could find beauty in an ashtray. I love doing that in my own work whether through extending beams to grab air or frame the sky, or using such materials as rammed earth, crushed glass, or glass pharmaceutical bottles composed into chandelier bubbles of "raining" light (page 89). All that is about finding the beauty in something familiarly mundane and to looking at things in new ways. I pay attention to detail and circumstance. Nothing is random. There is freedom and there is discipline. For example, the client for whom I designed the chandelier out of pharmaceutical bottles owns a pharmaceutical company. You see, there is a direct connection. I am looking for an anomaly. Once I see, I begin to think, "How can I use that in a beautiful way?"

VB Is the intention of looking for an anomaly to discover a path to designing something that no one has ever seen before?

EJ That would be a compliment, but it is never a motivation. If people are delighted, amazed, and surprised, that's a wonderful compliment. But the reason I do it is to add substance, to add stories. I usually have a story behind every solution. There is always a reason. It is like going to an art exhibit. You see something interesting and it may be quite incomprehensible until you read about it, and once you discover the story behind it you may relate to it and even understand yourself better. I only thought of using those pharmaceutical bottles when I saw a whole pallet of them in my client's warehouse. I said, "We absolutely have to do something about that!"

VB In your work I also noticed such inspirations as hawks and wings in how the roofs are put together. Could you talk about your inspirations for those? Could you talk more about how the "Prairie Chicken" house inspired your "Prairie Raptor" house? You said, "Two-by-twelve boards lapped like the feathers on a giant predator bird."

EJ First, you have to understand the scale of the place. It is 40 acres of wooded landscape sloping down towards the city, miles in the distance. It is different from being in the city where you would have a quarter of one acre. And it is Oklahoma where architecture tends to be high pitched roofs, brick, and wood shingles. It would be inappropriate to use that particular combination of materials in Arizona, Montana, Oregon, Mexico, or other places where I typically work. Therefore, I was very eager to use those common Oklahoma materials. How could I transform something ordinary into something extraordinary? And then I had the "Prairie Chicken" house in my head for half a century! It had to manifest somehow. And considering the generosity of the land, the house needed to reach out in all directions to scoop up the landscape and air; to spread its wings. It is a house with two long axes, about 200 feet long each and perpendicular to one another. They can't just terminate arbitrarily. One needs to have a story. The tallest thing in Oklahoma is the Devon Tower built for Big Oil in downtown Oklahoma City, which is visible from the site, so I aimed the primary axis of the house at that tower (page 90). The predator was aiming at Big Oil, not the "Prairie Chicken." [Laughs.] When I set up these view corridors, I end them with a gift! That was the start. It was a very special project. Three African Serval cats, speedy and graceful, with very long, sharp teeth, share their occupancy with the owners. So, the architecture intends to emulate their speed and grace. That was definitely an anomaly to design a house for wild cats, as opposed to children. So the more unusual the program, the better. I thrive on unusual programs. That said, all projects contain anomalies. Some are more apparent than others.

VB How would you define your work – American, regional, vernacular?

EJ Well, I have spent my life avoiding answering that question. I don't want to define my work that way. And if you look at it, especially houses, there is quite a range of responses. For example, two of my wife Lisa and my own houses – one in Phoenix, the other in Puerto Peñasco, Mexico – are completely different. Casa del Nido Osprey (page 198) is inserted into undulating dune on the coast of the Sea of Cortez. The design is influenced by local architecture with self-supporting brick domes, which are laid entirely by hand. Their precision was verified by the naked eye of an exceptionally gifted local builder, Plinio Rivera. The house in Phoenix (page 288) is anchored to its site by rammed earth. The barn-like central living space is surrounded by petal-like outdoor cylindrical courtyards. The circular geometry came from the nearby 40 foot diameter neighborhood water chlorination tank. To most people this would be an eyesore. For me it became a key design reference… the mother cylinder. The main butterfly roof channels all rainwater to the elliptical stair tower graced by a prominently placed scupper to celebrate the rain event and direct water to the landscape for irrigation. As Antoine Predock once said, "my regionalism is portable."

VB I am curious how you would respond to some of your own quotes that I found in your texts and interviews. Perhaps you could elaborate somewhat.

EJ Go ahead.

VB You said, "I've been very successful in 'selling' my designs, because I ground them in fundamentals."

EJ I want all of my designs to be defended by practicality, yet, they must have a poetic component. If it is only poetic it is not finished. If it is only pragmatic it is not finished. It must be both.

VB "Buildings have to inspire us. They have to enrich our lives. Otherwise, we'll throw them away."

EJ As Kahn said, "Buildings shelter mankind and architecture shelters the spirit of mankind." Isn't that the least we can do in return for having the privilege of calling ourselves architects? I want every community to be better because of the building we put there. If we don't care, no one will be compelled to care. When I used to give lectures on sustainability, I would open with a slide of Fallingwater. Why? That house leaks like a sieve. It is cold in the winter and it is hot and humid in the summer, and it costs a fortune to run and maintain. But it is sustainable because it is so beautiful; we love it and we will not allow it to be thrown away. I never want my students to forget beauty and enrichment is as important as energy conservation. How many sustainable buildings have we seen that are clunky, oppressive, and kill the sidewalk? So, what if they have a low utility bill? Who is benefiting from these buildings? When one constructs a building, every site is, in a sense, destroyed. So, I feel the weight of environmental responsibility to respect the act of destroying a little bit of the planet in order to improve something else. We better be kind and gentle to that precious site. I don't believe in people owning land; we are here only to take care of it. But having said that, I am not worrying about the planet because she will take care herself. She has millions of years to repair the damage we are doing. Humans may become extinct, but the planet will be fine.

VB "It's great when you're naïve, because there's no fear." You talked about this gift of yours earlier.

EJ Yes, it is my greatest asset. The lure of delight, excitement, and experimentation overwhelms the focus on what could go wrong. And honestly, rarely does something actually go wrong. For example, when we designed the "House of Five Dreams" (page 268), we did a curved glass wall in the living room. A ¼-inch thick, 3-inch-wide stacked glass wall – 27 feet tall and 75 feet long; totally self-supporting. The only thing holding it up is its undulating geometry. No professional glazing contractor would have anything to do with it. So, we ended up hiring bicycle mechanics to build it. They were patient and they were naïve. That's how we built it and it is beautiful. I visit that space often. I am still friends with all my residential clients.

VB And finally, "Obscure the separation between built and natural. Nature is painting the house; she is finishing the house for us."

EJ I think this is a good place to mention the work of Andy Goldsworthy, one of my favorite artists, a British sculptor, photographer, and environmentalist who produces site-specific sculptures and land art situated in nature. I admire him for his ability to give nature voice using natural materials as nature's vocabulary. His work usually disappears with little remaining or no trace at all. He will go into the forest or field and wait for inspiration. In the forest, he sees twigs everywhere. He starts building a twig dome (page 157). He finishes and takes a photograph. He returns a week later, then another week later, and so on taking additional photos. After just one season, it is gone. The Earth has completely consumed it without leaving a mark. Or he might build a series of stone arches on a beach during low tide (page 158). As the tide comes in, he takes a photo. Just eight hours later the tide will take the durable stone structure and dismantle it. But you will see some stones left. That describes all our favorite ruins. The Parthenon had a wooden roof and it is long gone. What's left? The stone.

VB Here are some of the words that you use to describe your architecture: alignments, proximity, craftsmanship, calmness, refinement, easy, and mystery. What other single-term words would you use to describe your work or the kind of architecture that you are trying to achieve?

EJ This is something that has eluded me all my life, and I am still working on it. And that is "restraint." To name one living architect who is influencing me today, it would have to be Peter Zumthor. I went to see his Kolumba Museum in Cologne, Germany. It was the refinement and restraint that struck me the most with its simplicity, elegance and beauty. I want to do that, and I want to be that good. It seems like a complete contradiction – to be fascinated with Goff and Zumthor at the same time. But somehow, I love both. Restraint is difficult. It takes a lot of skill.

VB How would you describe the intention of your work? Apart from refinement, restraint, elegance, and simplicity what is it that you are trying to achieve in your architecture?

EJ I don't want to make a mistake. I want my design decisions to succeed. I am not designing pie in the sky, or form for form's sake. I will not use another material just for the experience of using another material. No, I want the expectations of myself, my client, and my community to be fulfilled. Whatever it takes, those are my intentions. And having that attitude almost always results in exceeding expectations.

VB Finally, what is your view of the current creative climate in Arizona or more broadly in the Southwest?

EJ I am very optimistic… without hesitation. The great thing about working in Arizona, as opposed to Los Angeles or New York, is we are a big family of architects. We have very good architects such as Rick Joy, Michael Johnson and Wendell Burnette, to name the ones with wider reputations. Their work is consistently outstanding. There is Antoine Predock and Bart Prince in Albuquerque, New Mexico. More importantly, there is a new generation of men and women architects who worked for each of us and are now practicing independently doing excellent work. Keep an eye on Matt and Maria Salenger of coLAB Studio, more importantly, as Neal and I respectfully embrace our slow drift towards death, you will see our young partners, Brian and Jacob, soar beyond us! Additionally, there is a true, authentic social consciousness to these young architects, and the recognition politics is important. There is a will to get involved in leading communities where they work and live. I think an architect would make the best city counselor, mayor, governor, or city planner because we can remain objective problem solvers in most political situations. What are we doing as architects if we can't affect local public policy? I am very proud to be a part of my city's development. Ever since I came to Phoenix it's been on the cusp. It's always… becoming. There was a time when it was growing, sprawling, chewing our beautiful desert and spitting it out in the name of capitalism. But we matured in a smart way and we don't do that anymore thanks to the voices of the enlightened. I see an incredible commitment in our younger generation demanding design excellence for this incredible city in the desert. Our extreme summer temperatures come from great potential radiating heat!

Unbuilt

Casa Della Sfere / 2017
Crater House / 2016
Phoenix Tower / 2018

"His intuitive edge shares an inspiring perspective overlooked in plain sight yet unveiling truths – revealing a sense of place so appropriate."

"Eddie exists in the 4th dimension and perceives meaning beyond the obvious. His constant grin reminds us of Alice in Wonderland's Cheshire Cat – curiously provoking you into a perplexing and philosophical conversation."

John Grable

FAIA (John Grable Architects, Inc.).

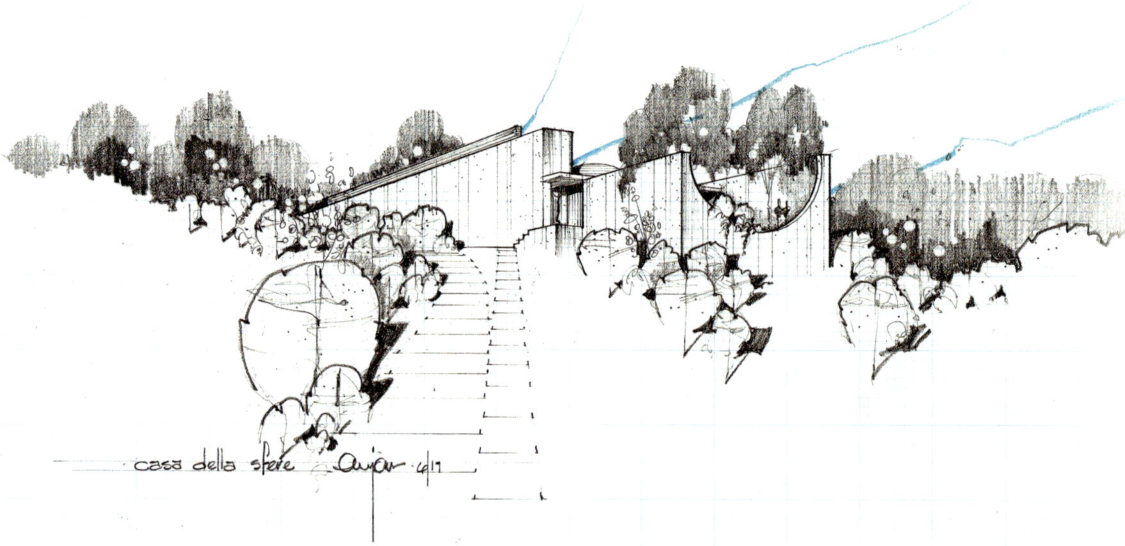
casa della sfere
6/17

casa della sfere
6/17

Casa della Sfere - A Fantasy

Milwaukee, Wisconsin

/ 2017

Just when you thought I was gone, I'm back.

Though my intentions are pure, you may see me as a pest. Perhaps I am! But I am also an architect who is compelled to put ideas on paper regardless of outcome. You can imagine how liberating it must be to not self-impose an expectation on a creative impulse.

I only saw your site survey for a few minutes. It showed a very long, deep, narrow site sloping up from the street, with what I can imagine, is an exceptional view of Lake Michigan.

That's it. No address, no Google earth, no program, no slope information, not even one dimension. What I had was my imagination, broad assumptions and a spontaneous thought for an architecture of restraint and mystery. Although I don't know you like an architect needs to know you, I drew from our time together last March and made up the rest!

Based on such limited site information, creating the design was extremely rewarding and challenging. I am happy to share my drawings if you would like to see them.

But first… the story.

It's morning in Milwaukee: blue sky, summer relenting to fall. A typical slow Sunday drive along the lakeshore is suddenly interrupted. How many times have we admired the vast distance of the lake and not noticed the strange form high on the hill, opposite the water?

It appears strange only in contrast to the grand mansions on either side. Unlike these magnificent symbols of history and old wealth, the unusual structure is both past, present, and future. Just as a whisper can be heard above noise, the subject of our attention cannot be ignored. It appears self-aware and confident in its simplicity. It gives away nothing. The architecture beckons but the entry approach is ambiguous.

It seems we can park here and ascend the hill using subtle cuts in the slanted grade. The closer we get, the more fortified the structure becomes. It must be a castle, a contemporary castle, but it is impossible to date.

Ah, stairs. We recognize stairs along the mid-face of a very long solid wall which disappears into the slope in one direction and thrusts forward towards the lake in the other. At the top of the stair is a recognizable classic sculpture standing guard near a large wooden panel. The wood signals the possibility of a door. We are intimidated.

Suddenly, the wood wall pivots, straddling the thick concrete. A beautiful woman is standing on the other side. Her name is Mary. She smiles in reaction to our astonished expressions and welcomes us into a secret garden. We step in. Relief turns to amazement. Where are we? Are we inside? Are we still outside?

No matter, conventional notions of home and shelter become irrelevant. We learn from Mary this place is called "Casa della Sfera." I think the name is misleading because we are surrounded by unapologetic orthogonal geometry. Why an Italian reference to a sphere? Our attention is drawn to an ethereal green light. The kind of light only passed through translucent leaves. It is deeper into the building and balances the more direct light from the garden. In the other direction, towards the lake, further away, we notice a distinguished older gentleman facing away from us and lost in thought: lost in a view better writers have described as being the "space between heaven and earth."

Mary invites us to follow her into an area furnished for conversation and infrequent entertainment. Above, a large circular cut out in the concrete ceiling exposes a beautiful corbeled brick bóveda. At its apex, a cross-shaped sliver of light prevents its geometric completion.

We are distracted by an amber glow flickering within a recess in the heavy concrete wall. It is

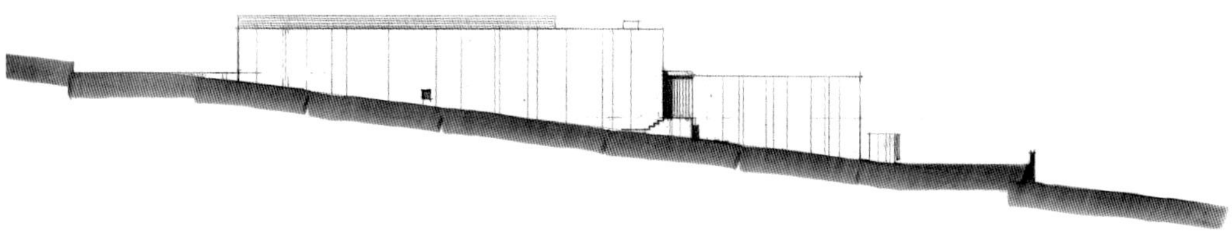

a familiar dancing light, typically produced by flame. The recess resembles a fireplace but we cannot see the fire: only the residual result and an occasional spark. The image is compelling, so we move into the recess. There it is; the fire hunkered even deeper into what feels primeval. We don't ask why the traditional hearth has been re-interpreted as a feeling rather than its usual symbol of family togetherness.

Turning, we see a private stairway going up. It is not clear what it is for. It's stark and long; walls, ceiling and floor are one material; it is dimly lit. At the top is an even longer corridor. Its proportions rarely encountered in any structure, anywhere.

It occurs to us, one must walk into the fireplace to find the hidden stair.

Beyond we can see more reflected light. This time, its intensity signals a large source of daylight. We are reminded of being lost in a labyrinth of medieval hill town passageways. We search for the turn with the most daylight flowing between corner buildings indicating the location of the public square.

We proceed down the corridor toward the light and are rewarded with, not a public square, but the most private and removed area so far. We see another garden, only this time it is an eye level landscape of treetops. Beyond the treetops, our confused orientation is reset once we understand the elevated view of the lake.

We sense it is time to go. Grateful for the unique tour, we return to the secret garden. Before we pass for the last time through the concrete wall, we notice the sound of trickling water. It takes a second glance but our eyes confirm a thin slot in the pavement with water flowing towards the downhill, towards the infinity of Lake Michigan. It is coming from inside the dwelling, passing under our feet, settling in the circular pool then emerging again to disappear into the faint blue intersection of sky, horizon and water.

We say goodbye to our proud hostess. Looking past her sincere smile we see the older man still content with his thoughts and special place. He knows he's home.

Days later, walking alone, I had not stopped thinking about that house. I was satisfied still having open questions, preferring to let the experience be a collection of memory and mystery.

However, the name "Casa della Sfere" remained an unresolved riddle. The architecture had been unrelenting and severe, sharp planes with ninety degree corners. I recall a couple of circles but not a sphere. I supposed an architecture of this sophistication may not be literal, so maybe the namesake was hidden; maybe hidden yet appearing obvious once its secret was revealed. Maybe it's not whole. Maybe the sphere is in separate pieces. Two pieces? Three pieces?

Yes, there could be three pieces. I think I know.

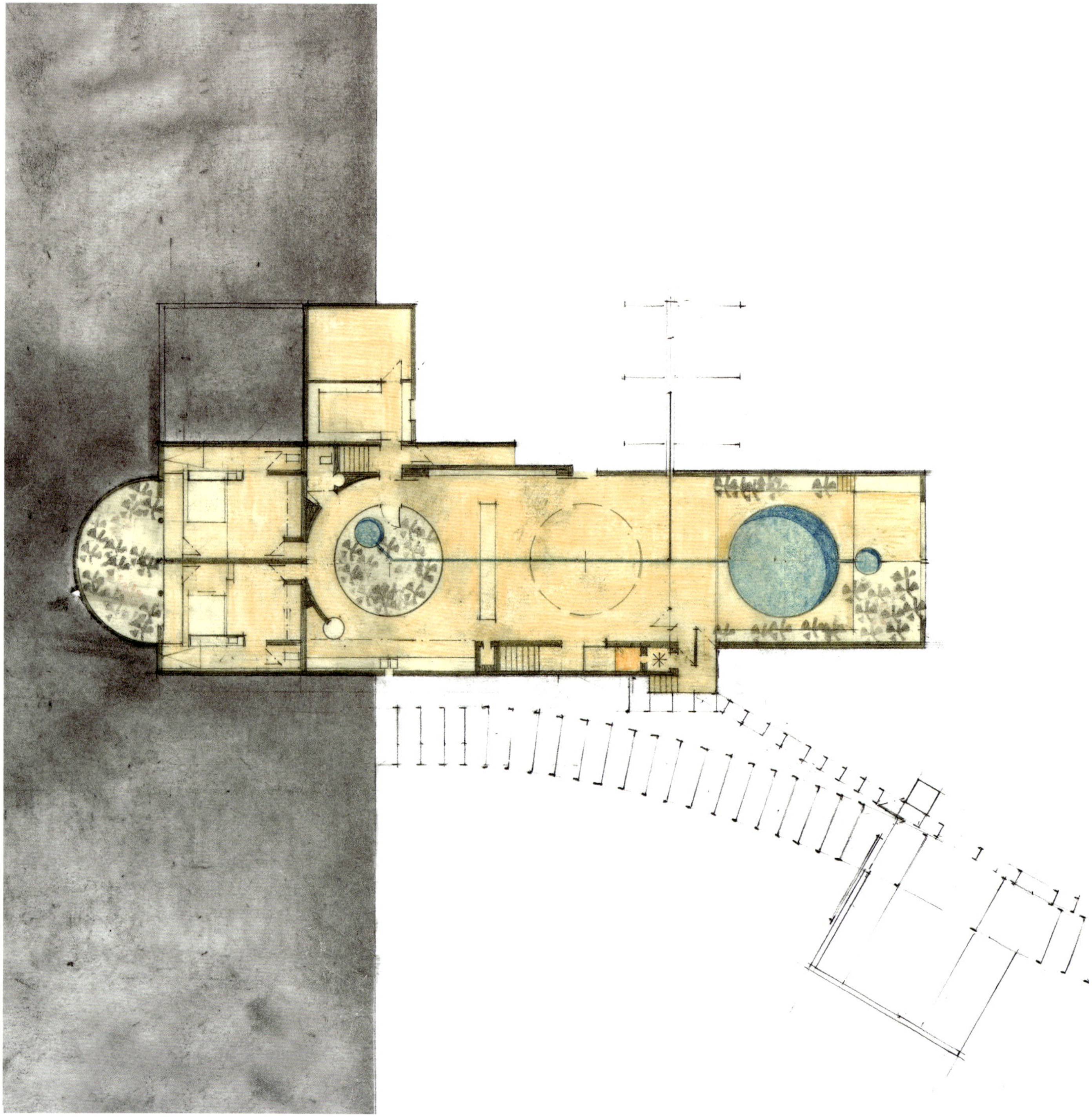

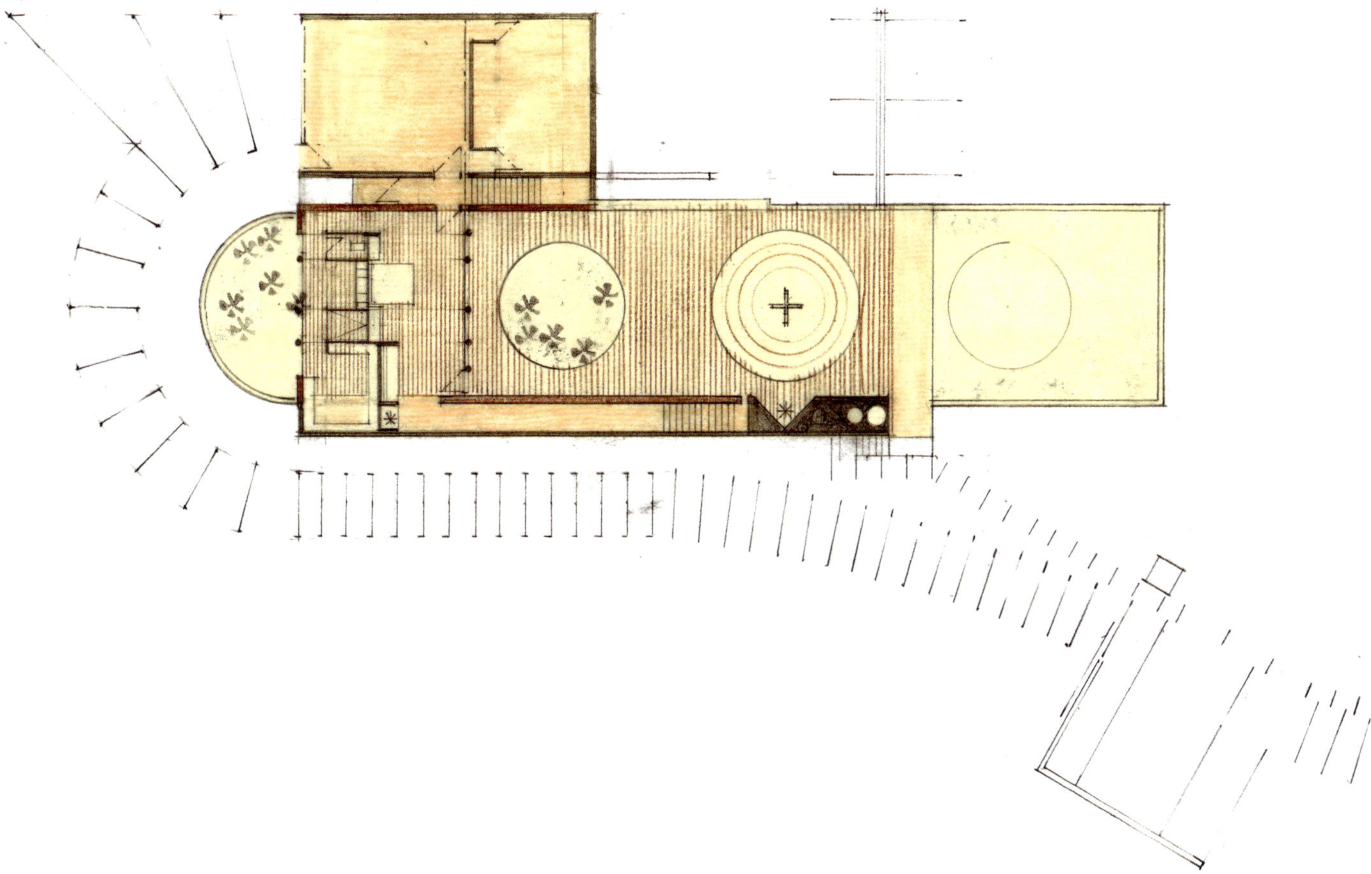

"Rather than impose a plan upon the landscape, it was decided to work in phase with the surroundings… but it will be worked enough so the desired experience will be heightened and ordered. This could also allow the piece to exist without beginning or end."

James Turrell

Artist and architect. 2009 Fellow of the Royal Institute of British Architects, London, England. 2013 National Medal of Arts.

Turrell, James. Roden Crater (sunset). 2010. Gagosian Gallery, London. Kwon, Miwon. Rooms for Light, Light on Its own. London, Gagosian Gallery, 2011.

Crater House

Coconino County, Arizona
/ 2016

The following collection of concept drawings is a personal architectural tribute to March 15, 2016. James Turrell is one of the world's most important artists and though I'd had several opportunities over the years to introduce myself, I never did. I was too shy! So, when my Arizona studio phone rang on an early Monday morning, I was understandably amazed. I heard Mr. Turrell asking if I could meet him in northern Arizona... for lunch... tomorrow... the fifteenth of March.

Sure!

His timing could not have been better. I had, for the past several months, been working on a residential compound masterplan in which I proposed a Turrell "SKYSPACE." This was my chance to explore the possibility. I invited Bill Osborne, a studio colleague, to bring his laptop along so we could show Mr. Turrell the masterplanned acreage in 3D.

We arranged to meet at the Beaver Street Brewery in downtown Flagstaff. Mr. Turrell arrived, we shook hands, ordered lunch and as suddenly as his Monday morning phone call... he became "James" to me.

So it began...

We discussed many things including the SKYSPACE, but one subject of particular importance and the reason for his call, was his idea to construct six houses by six architects spread far apart on a bluff overlooking Roden Crater. Each home would be commissioned by an individual family interested in living two months each year in the presence of the crater, while the remaining ten month program would convert to an artist-in-residence.

Having completed our first meal together, James suggested we tour Roden Crater and look at possible sites. He asked, "Would you have time?" Meaning, would I have time to tour what has been called "the most anticipated public art installation of the twenty-first century?"

Sure!

The next six hours were among the most extraordinary of my life.

Nearly anyone who has seen Turrell's multi-decade project photographs will agree, the completed elements are extremely provocative and beautiful but difficult to understand. Even with James' explanation and the benefit of standing in Roden's physical space, Bill and I had to make every effort to retain the stampede of complex technical information that was competing with his soaring aspirations. This, plus an overwhelming amount of visual stimulus, left us dizzy but inspired.

Nightfall was coming when we took the big truck on top of the crater rim. James used his finger to point at possible home building sites. Was he kidding? After hours of solar system majesty, planetary phenomenon and the precise mathematical angles of celestial view vectors, I was simply looking down the index finger of James Turrell to locate my site... about one and a half miles off in the fading distance! I attempted a mental photograph.

As the sun began its spectacular setting, James turned us east. He taught me there is no such thing as nightfall. There is only night rise.

He was right, of course. That evening, Bill and I learned how to see again. We were witnesses to a rising pale blue sky forming a pink crescent with subtle grey shadow rays radiating from the arc of night. That March day, with its equal evening partner, struck a match inside my head, fuzzy with age but still protected by an open heart.

I would soon experience another example of good timing.

A family trip to Italy's Amalfi Coast had been planned for mid-June, a few months later. Before I was to leave, I assembled all the topographic information I could download off satellite imagery and geological mapping. When the time came, I rationalized my mental photograph could accurately locate the site on axis with the long dimension of Roden's elliptical cone.

I wanted this project. I could not wait for a formal commission. I was about to live in a 600-year-old Italian villa for thirty days. My view: the mythical Isle of Capri… the land of Ulysses, Sirens, and Homer's Odyssey, an island surrounded by the brilliant azure water of the Tyrrhenian Sea.

I expected this month-long experience to be profoundly inspirational. I could not be idle. I determined the first iteration of Crater House would be a response to logical assumptions rather than the reality of an actual client. I based my brief on a normal residential program: living space, food preparation, dining, entertaining, main bedroom and guest rooms. In addition, I'd include a specific artist studio, a writing space, and other residential components convertible to flexible studio

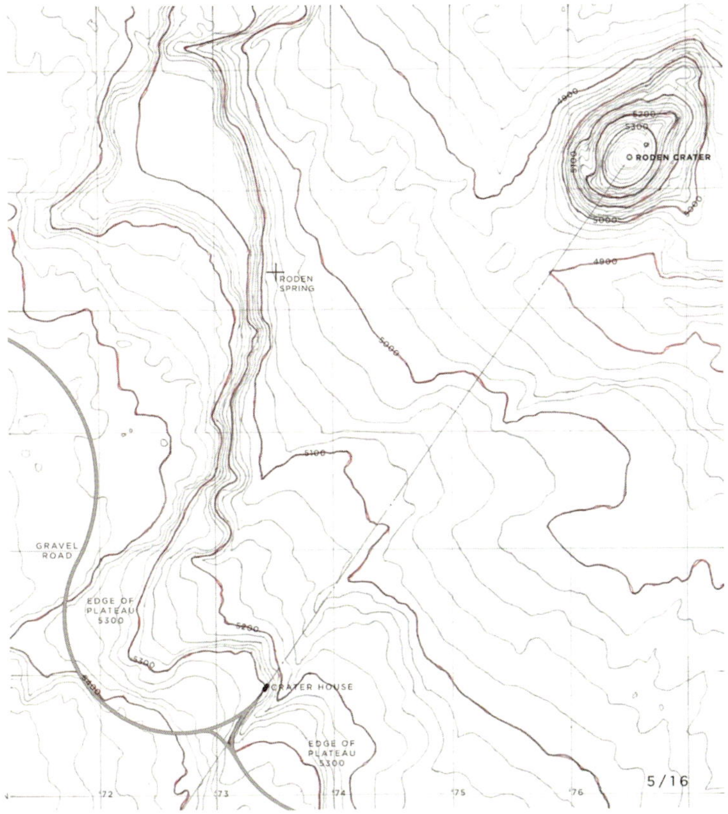

RODEN CRATER
RODEN SPRING
GRAVEL ROAD
EDGE OF PLATEAU 5300
CRATER HOUSE
EDGE OF PLATEAU 5300
5/16

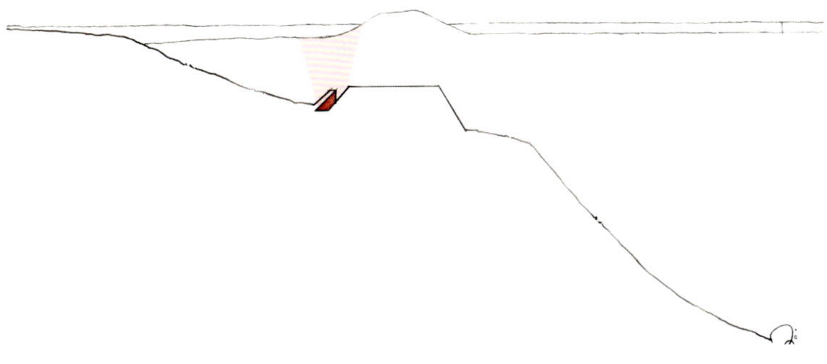

work areas both indoor and outdoor. Though the image of Roden Crater is undeniably profound, I decided it was best to provide an artist in residence respite from its powerful reputation. Therefore, the upper level studio is strategically located to focus sight lines downward to undisturbed high-desert foreground at the bluff's base.

Conceptually, the home's design is meant to project ambiguity. Is it modern? Is it classic? Is it old or new? There is timelessness to thick masonry arches and a monolithic material palette. The house will exist in a modern world but sit peacefully in a vast 50,000 acre landscape of extinct volcanoes and cinder cones on the edge of Arizona's legendary Painted Desert. It is an architecture purposely subservient to nature. From the top of the bluff, it barely exists... a brief geometric interruption in a natural, ragged edge, set exactly level with the crater's rim. Once inside, there are choices. Introspective work? Or, approach the lower level's brick arch framing Turrell's earth intervention on the backdrop of a canopy of Arizona sky.

What if the month in Italy had not been in such close proximity to my first Turrell meeting?

But it was.

Drawing by Brian Andrews

I was surrounded by Italian architecture shaped by time. The image of Capri, solid in its continuously moving blue landscape, seemed more than similar to a crater landform anchoring another vast landscape. There is a special place inside Roden where one can look up through a razor thin cutout and perceive the true color of any daytime sky. The Tyrrhenian Sea reflects that color and becomes the sky! My drawings were made on an antique dining table surrounded by three foot thick stone walls radiating the aura of its most famous inhabitant, Caroline Bonaparte.

The month spent in Villa L'Annunziata was productive and inspiring. My architectural tribute became as much an exercise in the joy of hand drawing as it was a daydream without constraints. Would my proposed home design be different had I not been on the Amalfi Coast?

Sure!

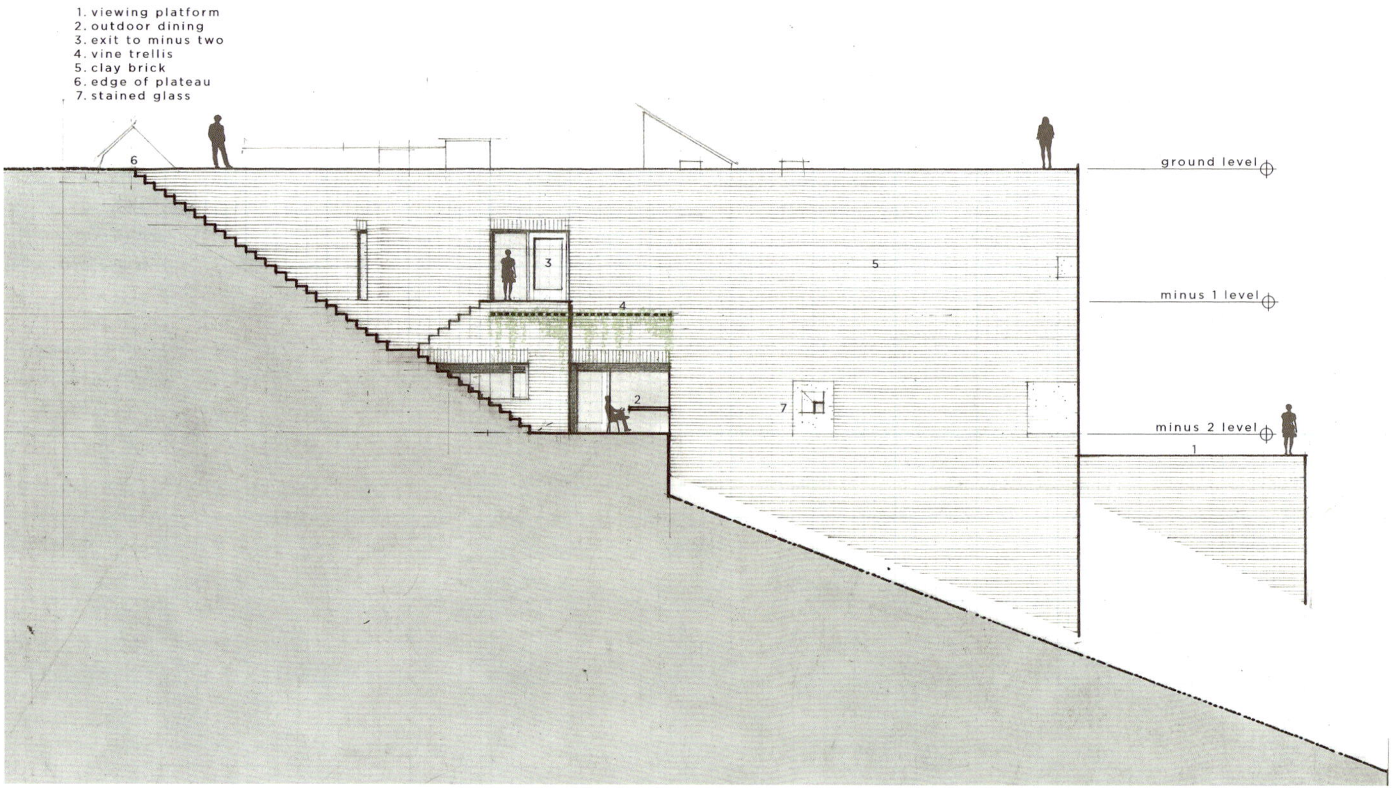
1. viewing platform
2. outdoor dining
3. exit to minus two
4. vine trellis
5. clay brick
6. edge of plateau
7. stained glass
ground level
minus 1 level
minus 2 level

1. minus one entry, translucent glass
2. minus two entry, solid wood
3. viewing platform
4. corner stone
5. brick pattern
6. clay brick

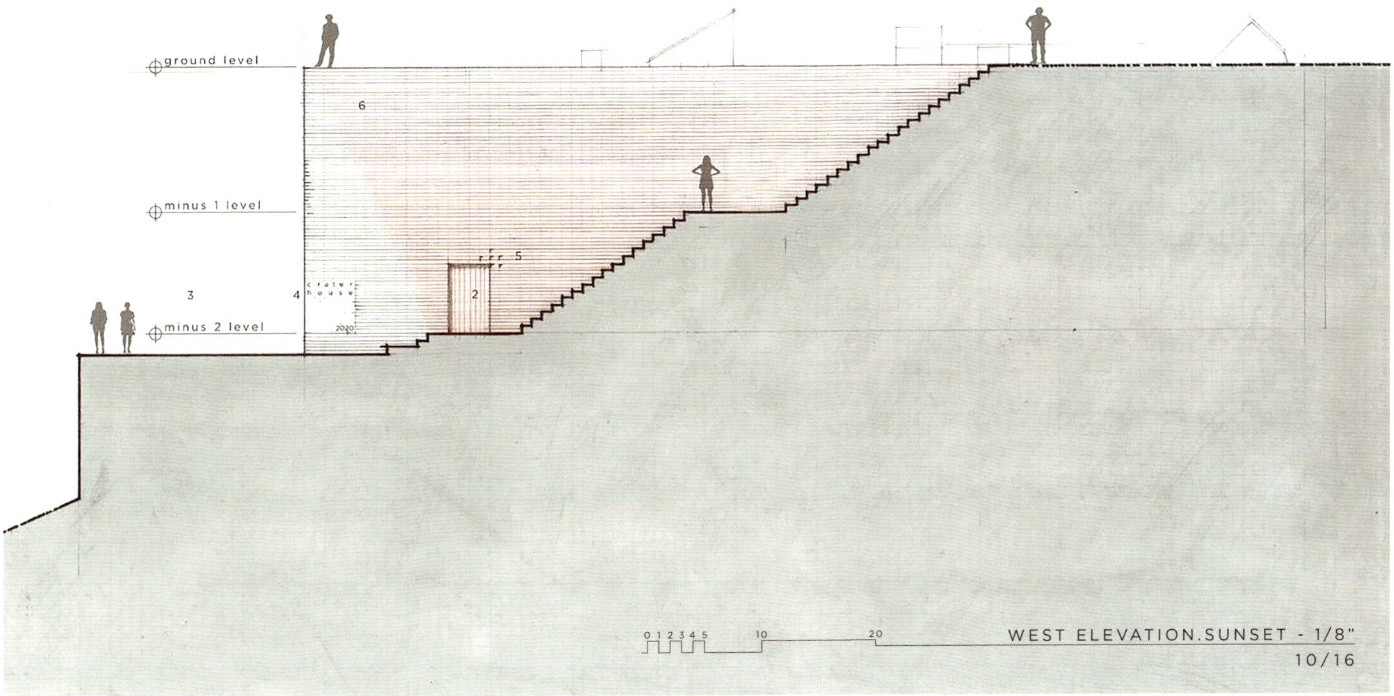

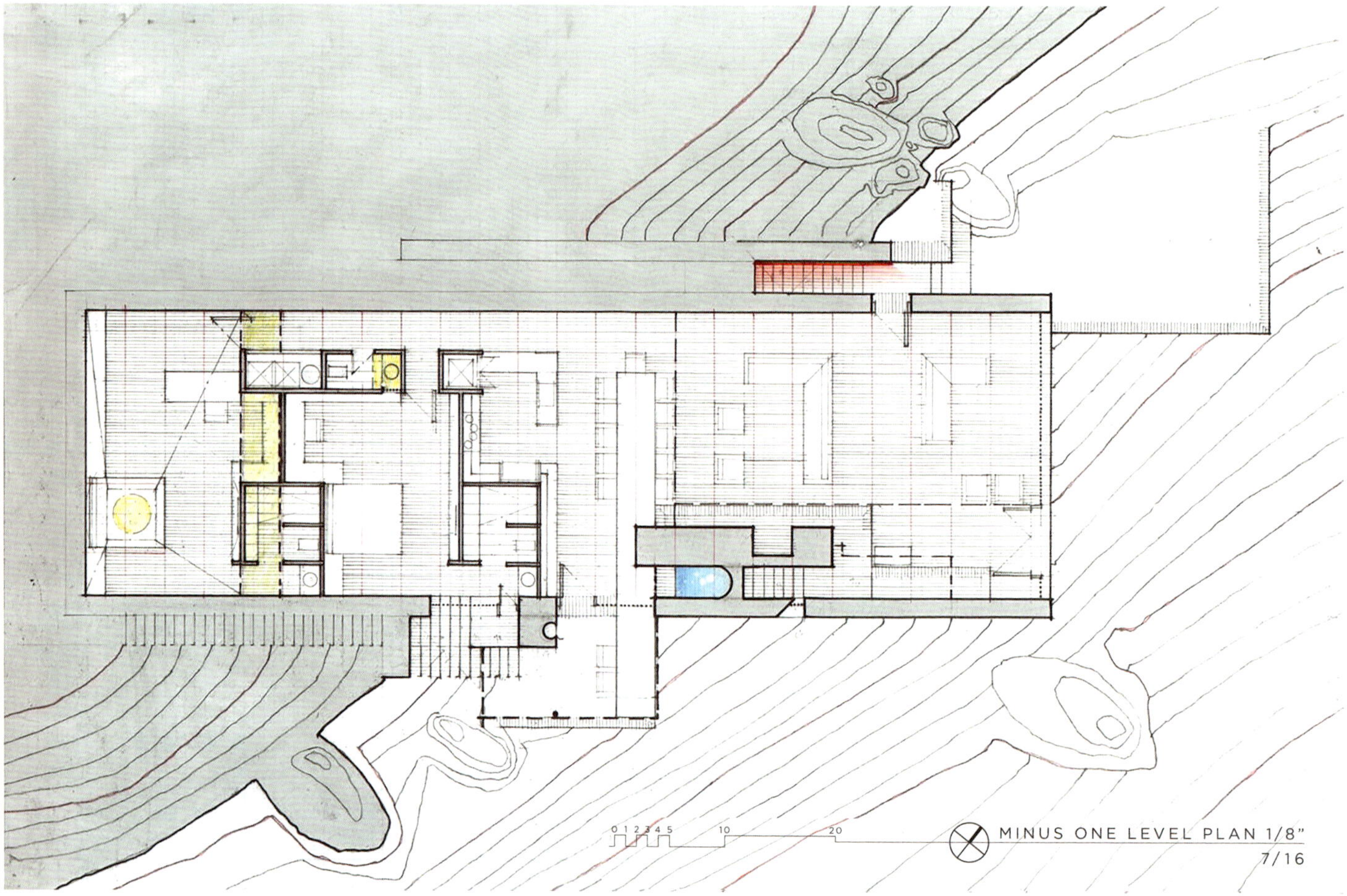
0 1 2 3 4 5
10
20
MINUS ONE LEVEL PLAN 1/8"
7/16

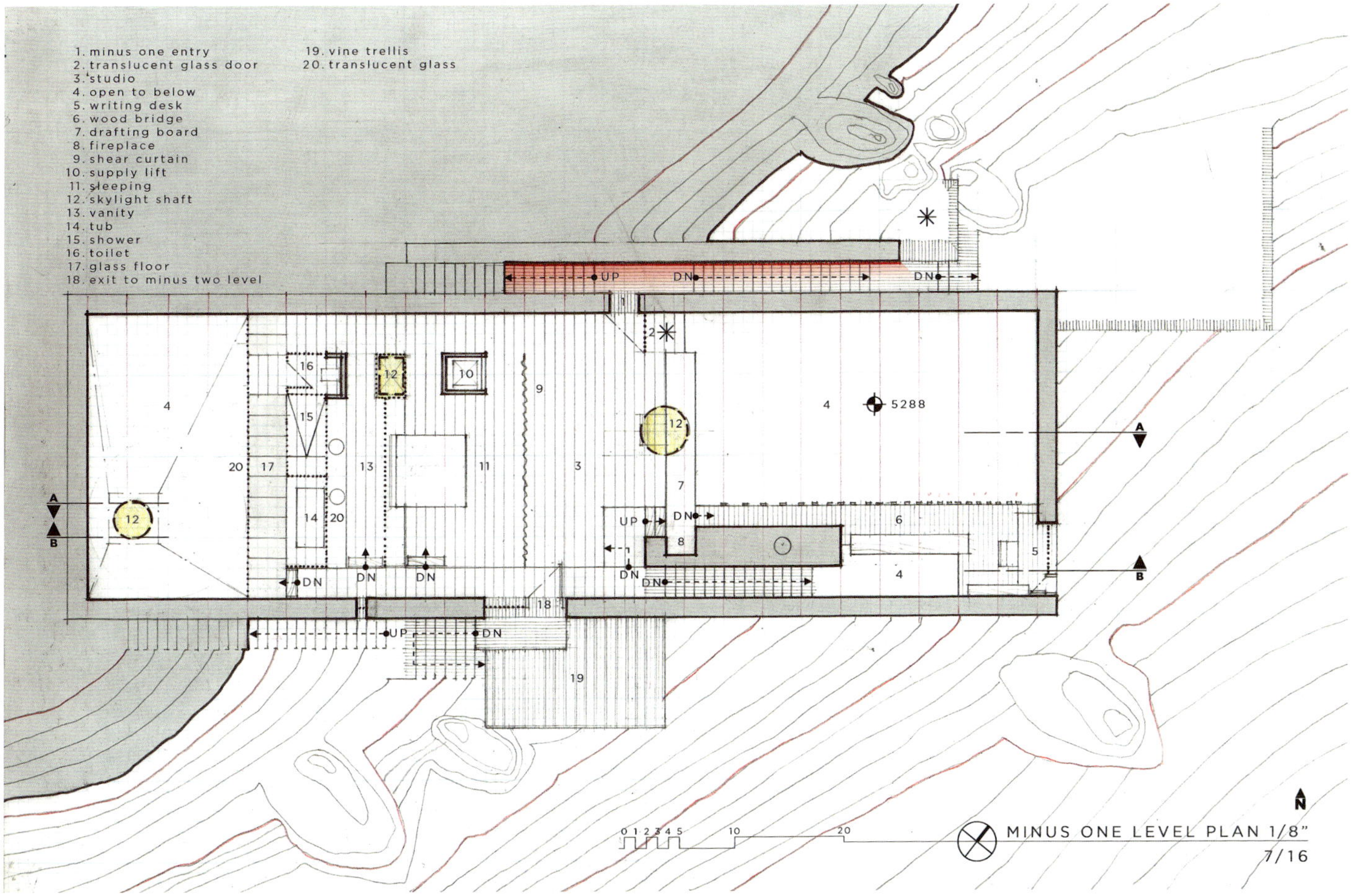
1. minus one entry
2. translucent glass door
3. studio
4. open to below
5. writing desk
6. wood bridge
7. drafting board
8. fireplace
9. shear curtain
10. supply lift
11. sleeping
12. skylight shaft
13. vanity
14. tub
15. shower
16. toilet
17. glass floor
18. exit to minus two level
19. vine trellis
20. translucent glass
MINUS ONE LEVEL PLAN 1/8"
7/16

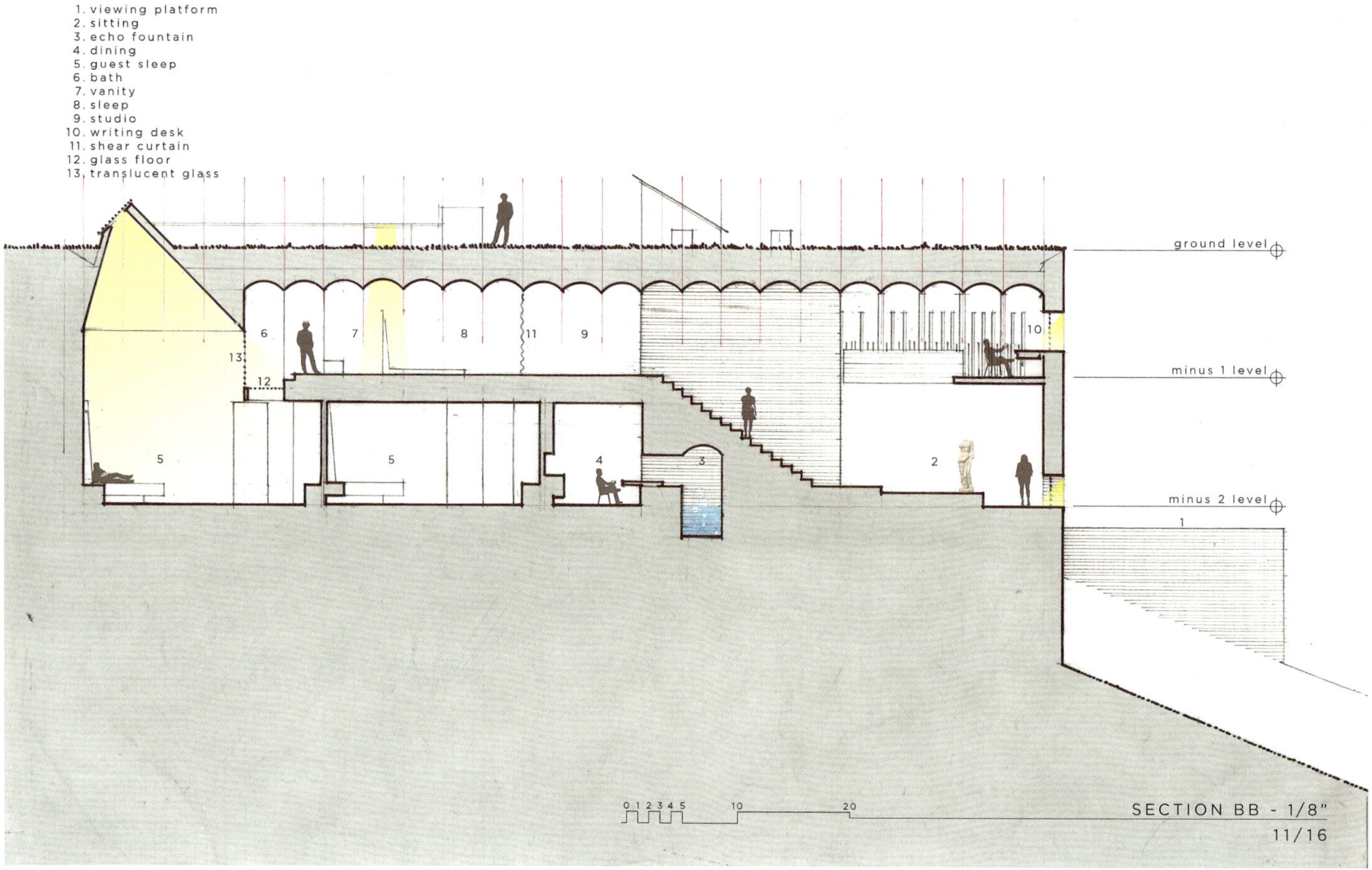
1. viewing platform
2. sitting
3. echo fountain
4. dining
5. guest sleep
6. bath
7. vanity
8. sleep
9. studio
10. writing desk
11. shear curtain
12. glass floor
13. translucent glass
ground level
minus 1 level
minus 2 level
0 1 2 3 4 5 10 20
SECTION BB - 1/8"
11/16

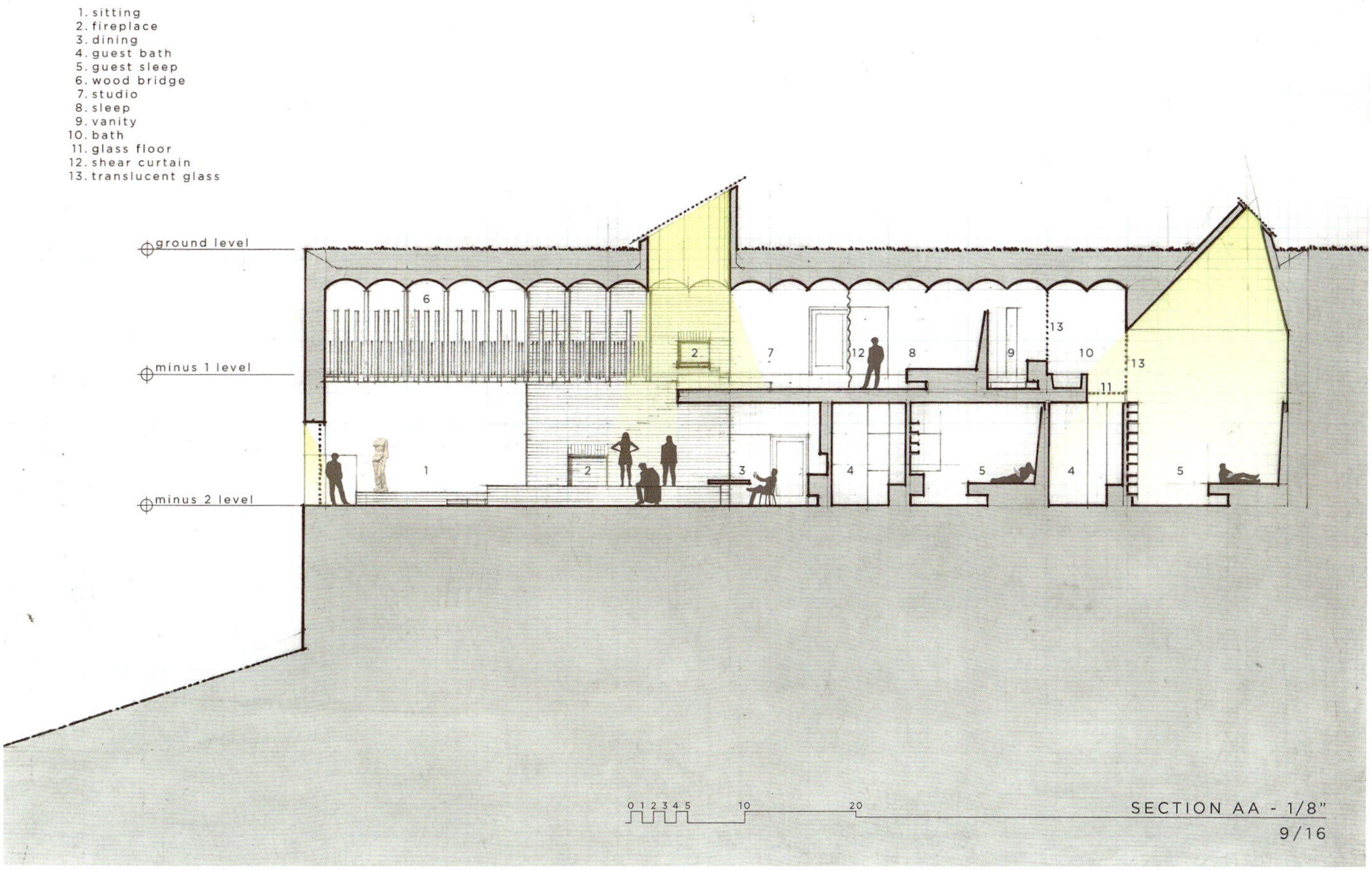
1. sitting
2. fireplace
3. dining
4. guest bath
5. guest sleep
6. wood bridge
7. studio
8. sleep
9. vanity
10. bath
11. glass floor
12. shear curtain
13. translucent glass
ground level
minus 1 level
minus 2 level
SECTION AA - 1/8"
9/16

16/16

2/16

"Eddie Jones is one of those immigrants to Arizona (in his case, from Oklahoma) who become one with the place in a way that natives like myself can only envy. His respect for – and understanding of – the desert has been matched by very few architects over the last 100 years, and the result is a body of work that redefines what modern can mean in this remarkable place."

Reed Kroloff

Dean & The Rowe Family College of Architecture Endowed Chair (Illinois Institute of Technology).

Phoenix Tower

Phoenix, Arizona
/ 2018

Houses in the sky

Let's assume minimizing demolition of small scale buildings constructed under antiquated economic scenarios is environmentally responsible and let's assume increased density is a necessary component for successful urban stability. We therefore need solutions for mixing historic/existing buildings with 21st century socioeconomic reality. The idea represented by this research is grounded in the expectation of an abundance of small urban sites in conflict with conventional developer expectations for return on investment… the transitional cusp before the next generation of urban economics.

Not since Louis Sullivan changed the rules of high rise construction in the late 19th century has there been significant innovation in public policy recognizing the urbanistic possibilities of a steel bearing frame.

One option is to investigate a structural system capable of rising out of an inadequately-sized site with floor plates expanding once the structure clears the lower existing buildings. Other progressive adoptions would include the ownership of platform real estate encouraging individual architectural expression, interior volumetric choice and creative response to a broad range of programs.

This is an architecture that comes from pragmatic conditions yet is capable of accepting responsibility as a long awaited Phoenix icon recognizable around the world. The principal design solution is a response to site utilization, inevitable water shortages, a transitioning city, and is clearly adaptable to varying latitudes and global locations.

Of course, if one applies current zoning rules… the idea of a building hovering over an existing building or a height intersecting commercial flight paths... this architecture is completely illegal.

Time for a change! Phoenix says "follow me."

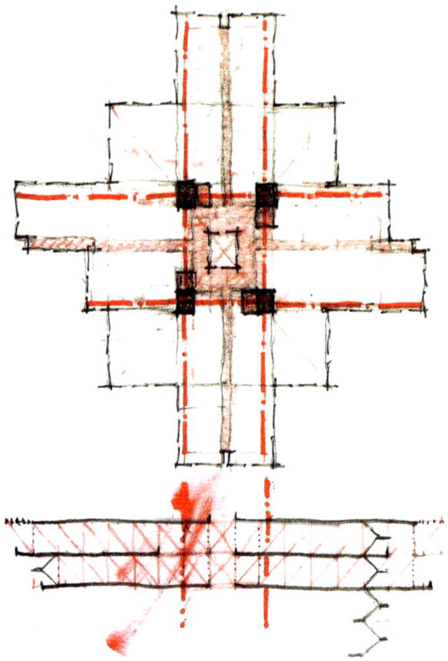

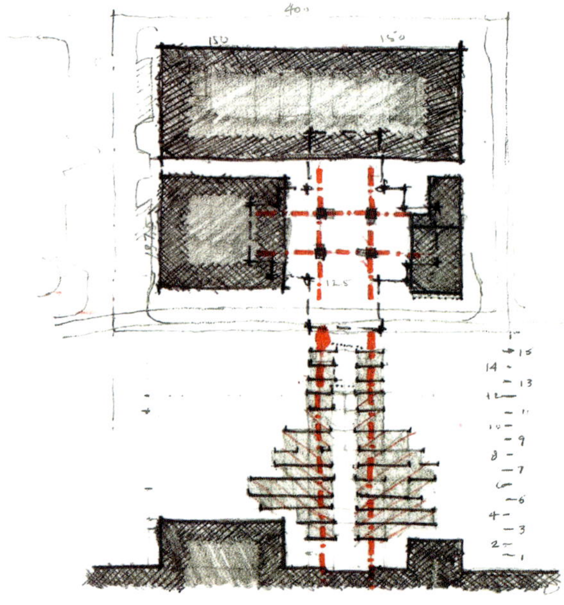

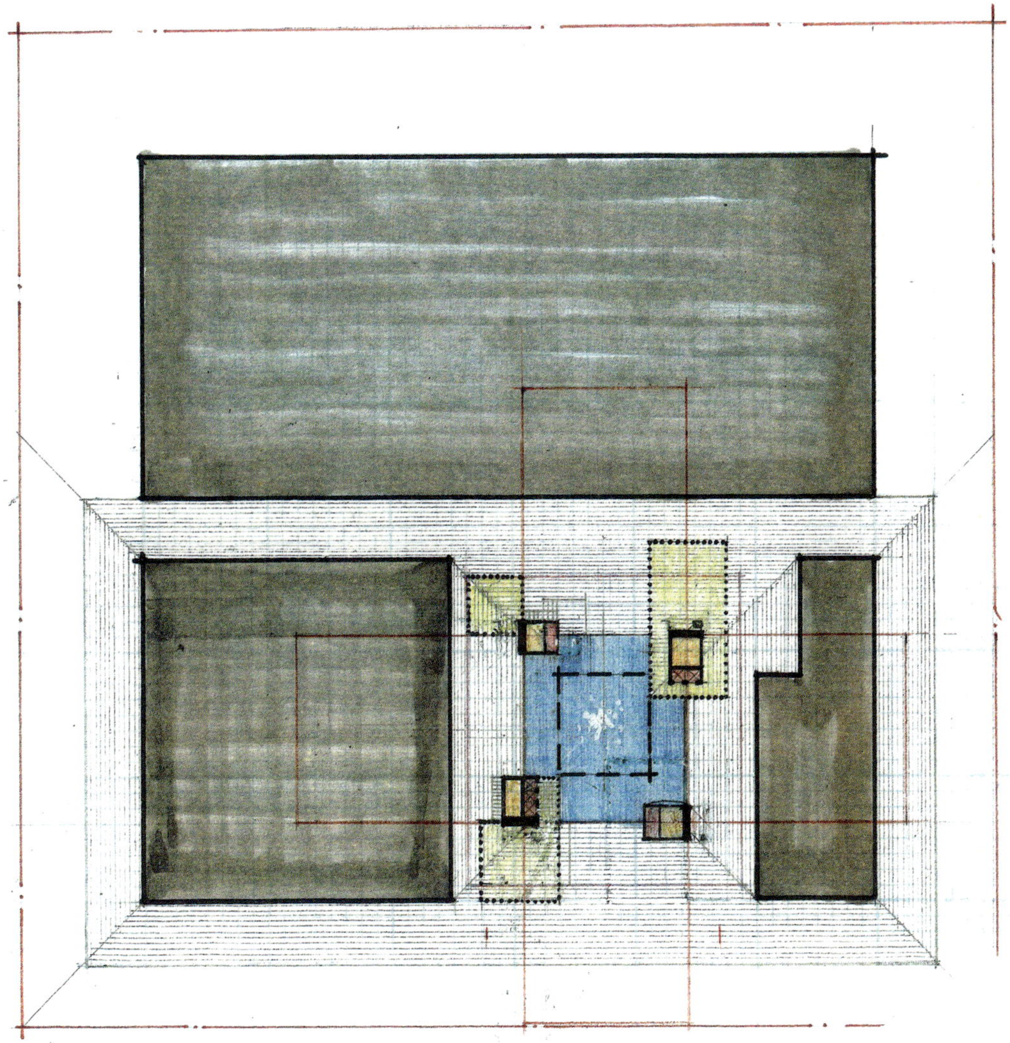

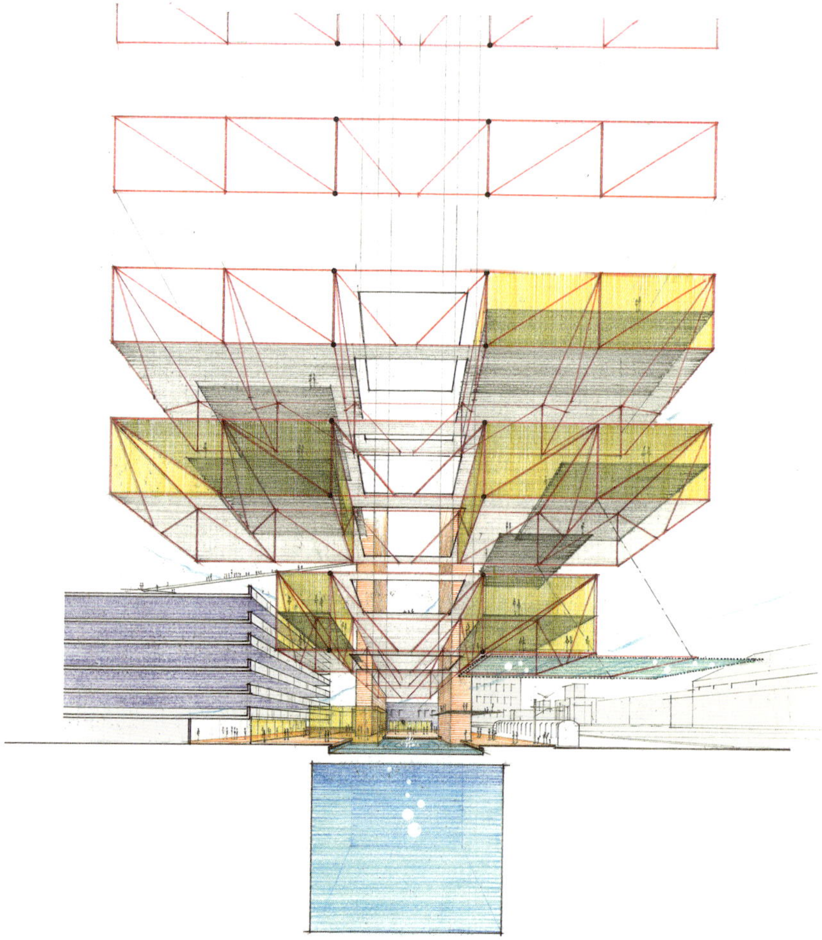

PHOENIX
landmark tower
TOWER PERSPECTIVE

Epilogue

by Eddie Jones

205

Writing in his influential 2003 book *Eero Saarinen, An Architecture of Multiplicity*, Antonio Romän examines Saarinen's perceived absence of interest in a so-called signature style. He concludes: "Saarinen's manifold quest might thus be summed up as an attempt to re-conceive modernism in response to contemporary diversity, as a search for unity within the condition of plurality."

I have never been one to overly intellectualize my work or architecture in general. However, Mr. Romän's assessment of Saarinen's motivation to explore a broad range of form, material and vernacular is one I, apparently, have embraced throughout my career. Avoiding easy categorization does not come without risking respect. Yet, I believe my work... Jones Studio's work... upholds a commitment to excellence and is a direct reflection of the individuality of our clients, their sites and broad range of program. I thrive on unique conditions and challenging constraints. I never know what will happen next.

I don't need to.

I don't want to.

Mies van der Rohe: "One doesn't invent a new architecture every Monday morning."

Architectural objectivity is an essential ingredient in the exploration of possibility and the discovery of creative, less obvious solutions. Although difficult, architecture has never felt like work!

Bruce Goff: "I must invent a new Architecture each time whether it's Monday morning or not."

Designers

Jones Studio

Family

Jones Studio is a mid-sized architecture, interior design, graphic design, public art, and planning firm founded in Phoenix 1979 by Eddie Jones, AIA. Younger brother Neal Jones, AIA joined the firm in 1986, and in 2014 Brian Farling, AIA and Jacob Benyi, AIA became principals and partners.

From the beginning, Jones Studio has created unique and memorable architecture that is a direct expression of the values and culture of those who occupy it and of the community in which it stands. They are widely respected as one of Arizona's most innovative architectural practices. With each project, they bring curiosity and commitment to provide the highest level of service to their clients. They believe architecture should be practiced with a respect for the earth, and that human ingenuity and creativity can shape our built environment for the better.

Jones Studio has received over two hundred design awards for over fifty projects. In 2014 Jones Studio was ranked 21st in the Architect 50 and 6th in the Sustainability Category. In 2016 the Mariposa Land Port of Entry received a National AIA Institute Honor Award, and in the same year was awarded a GSA Design Excellence Program Honor Award in Architecture. In 2011 Jones Studio was the recipient of the AIA Western Mountain Region's Firm of the Year Award.

Jones Studio has been recognized repeatedly for advancing sustainable design, including seventeen Arizona Forward Environmental Excellence Awards and six APS Energy Awards, and the Studio's ability to create strong teams has won five AIA Arizona Goodwin Awards for collaborative effort between the architect, contractor, and owner resulting in design excellence.

Since its start, the Jones Studio "family" has been a diverse team of highly motivated and enthusiastic creative professionals. "We thrive on the process of learning something new from each and every endeavor."

Eddie M. Jones, AIA, NCARB / Founder (1979)

It was morning, June 8, 1979. Instead of leaving for his day job with the oldest firm in Arizona, Eddie calmly stepped outside his home and glued eleven letters beside the door.

So began JONES STUDIO: in the spare bedroom, leaking roof, no money, and one brave client.

Five years later Eddie's younger brother, Neal, joined him, completing their childhood dream of working together and forever changing the scale of the practice.

Forty plus years forward, Eddie's persistence and innovation have expanded the palette of materials and methods available throughout Arizona. His long-standing implementation of sustainability and environmental design, matched with an extraordinary sensitivity to the factors that create space, have made better human experiences and better architecture.

Under Eddie Jones' leadership, Jones Studio has received 222 design awards including a National AIA and a GSA Design Excellence Honor for the Mariposa Land Port of Entry in Nogales, Arizona. In 2018 Eddie was awarded the AIA Arizona's Architects Medal, the highest honor an individual practitioner of architecture can receive in the state.

Eddie is a 2004 recipient of the Melvin R. Lohmann Medal (for career achievement in architecture) from his alma mater, Oklahoma State University. The Lohmann Medal is the highest honor bestowed on a graduate of the College of Engineering, Architecture, and Technology. Soon after, Eddie also became an inductee of the College of Engineering, Architecture, and Technology Hall of Fame. Although state rivals, the University of Oklahoma College of Architecture named Eddie the Bruce Goff Chair in 1999. For the fiftieth anniversary of the iconic Progressive Architecture Awards, he was specially selected to be a member of the esteemed jury.

Eddie was appointed in 2007 to the GSA Design Excellence Peer Review. He was named a Founding Board of Governors member by The School of Architecture at Taliesin in 2017. He is very active in Arizona Forward, Arizona's premier organization for promoting sustainable design. Eddie also hosts many community events at the new office building, completed in 2016 to serve as a model of sustainability in desert environments.

There are currently 40 books, 227 magazines and journals, 29 TV shows, various radio programs, one Hollywood movie and one documentary film including the Studio's works.

Recently, Eddie Jones realized his day job was again with one of the oldest firms in Arizona.

Book Credits

Photographer Credits
Key: Bill Timmerman (BT), Matt Winquist (MW), Robert Reck (RR), Jeremy Bitterman (JB), Ed Taube (ET), Tim Hursley (TH), James McGoon (McG), Mark Boisclair (MB), Larry Clements (LC), Mark Bryant (MBr), Alex Vertikoff (AV), Chris Winters (CW), Bill Tonnesen (BTo), Paul Markow (PM), Brian Farling (BCF), Brad Wheeler (BW), Aaron Eriksson (AE), Pere Planells (PP), Plinio Rivero (PR)

Cover: BT
Pages 2-3: BCF
Page 6: ET
Page 10-11: ET
Introduction: 19 – BW
Jones Studio: 26 – BT; 28-29 – ET; 32-33 – BT; 33 below – ET; 34-35 – BT; 36 upper – BCF; 36 below – BT; 37 – BCF; 38-39 – BT; 40-41 – MW; 42 – BT; 43 above – MW; 43 below – BCF; 44 above – BT; 44 below – MW; 45-49 – BT
Prairie Raptor: All BT; except 76 – LC
Singing Sands: All JB
Starwood: 120-127 – RR; 128 – MBr ; 129-133 – RR; 134 upper – MBr; 134 below – RR; 136-137 – MBr; 138 – RR; 139 – MBr; 140-141 – RR; 142-143 – MBr; 144-145 – MBr; 146-147 – MBr; 148-149 – MBr
Outpost: 152 – BT; 163 – RR; 164 – BT; 166 above – RR; 166 below – BT; 167-168 – BT; 171 – RR; 172 174 BT; 175 – RR; 176-177 – BT, 179 – RR, 180-193 – BT; 194-195 – RR
Casa del Nido Osprey: All RR; except 208 top right and below (Black & White) - PR
Logan Collection: 216 – RR; 218-219 – ET; 221 – RR; 222-223 – ET; 224 above – RR; 224 below – ET; 225-227 – RR; 228 – ET; 229 above left, above right, below right – ET; 229 below left – RR; 230 above – Bill Tonnesen; 230 below – RR; 231-236 – ET; 237 – RR; 238, 239 above and below – ET; 239 center – RR; 240-241 – ET; 242-243 – RR
Scorpion: 246 – MB; 249 – McG; 250-251 – MB; 252 – McG; 253 – MB; 254 – McG; 255 – MB; 256 above – McG, 256 below – MB; 257 – McG; 258-259 – MB; 260 – PP; 261 – McG; 262-263 – MB; 264-265 – PP
House of Five Dreams: All RR
Johnson Jones: 288-290 – TH ; 292-294 – ET; 296 – TH; 297 – AV; 298 – TH; 299 – AV; 301-305 above – TH; 305 below – AV; 306-307 – TH
Interview: 311 – AE; 316 – MBr
Phoenix Tower: 352 – MW
Epilogue: 360 – BT
Designers: 364 – PM
Pages 366-367: ET
Back Cover: RR

Contractor Credits
Jones Studio: BUILD Inc. – Rich Fairbourn (contractor), CW DESIGNS – Chris Winters (landscape architect)
Prairie Raptor: Construction Zone – Andy Byrnes, Michael Groves, Matt Muller
Singing Sands: Don Tankersley Construction – Don Tankersley
Starwood: Lentz Construction – John Lentz
Outpost: Construction Zone – Andy Byrnes, Michael Groves
Scorpion: Construction Zone – Andy Byrnes, Michael Groves
House of Five Dreams: Construction Zone – Andy Byrnes, Rich Fairbourn
Johnson Jones: Owner and Construction Zone

OSCAR RIERA OJEDA
PUBLISHERS

Art Direction: Oscar Riera Ojeda
Graphic Design: Kira Collins and Lucía B. Bauzá

ISBN 978-1-946226-44-0
Published by Oscar Riera Ojeda Publishers Limited
Printed in China

Oscar Riera Ojeda Publishers Limited
Unit 1003-04, 10/F.,
Shanghai Industrial Investment Building,
48-62 Hennessy Road, Wanchai, Hong Kong
T: +852-3920-9300

Production Offices | China
Suit 19, Shenyun Road,
Nanshan District, Shenzhen 518055
T: +1-484-502-5400

www.oropublishers.com | www.oscarrieraojeda.com
oscar@oscarrieraojeda.com